The Grolier Library
of
Environmental
Concepts and Issues

The Grolier Library of Environmental Concepts and Issues

Volume 4

Energy

Grolier Educational Corporation

SHERMAN TURNPIKE, DANBURY, CONNECTICUT 06816

Grolier Publishing Company,
Grolier Educational Corporation

Joseph Tessitore, Senior Vice President, Sales and Marketing
Robert R. Hall, Senior Vice President, Sales
Beverly A. Balaz, Vice President, Marketing
A. Joseph Hollander, Vice President and Publisher, School and Library Reference
Molly Stratton, Editor, School and Library Reference

M. E. Aslett Corporation
Michael Aslett, President
Jacqueline Flamm, Publisher
Rob Panco, Vice President

Published 1996 by
Grolier Educational Corporation
Danbury, Connecticut 06816

Published by arrangement with
M. E. Aslett Corporation
95 Campus Plaza
Edison, NJ 08837

ISBN 0-7172-7518-3
Library of Congress Catalog Number: 95-079112
Cataloging information can be obtained directly from Grolier Educational Corporation.
First Edition
Printed in the United States of America

Text pages and end sheets for this series printed on recycled paper.

STAFF

Project Director
Jennifer Copersino

Science Editor
Arnold Henderson

Editorial Director
Brenda Goldberg

Photo Editor
Vivian OKrepky

Art Imagers
Robert Bovasso
Brian Hewitt

Project Designer
Elizabeth Geary

Editors
James Aslett
Joan Aslett
Diane Frenick
Linda Speakman

Photo Researcher
Villette Harris

Electronic Imagers
Pat Caruso
Todd Koncsol
Phyllis Post
Michael Romeo

Illustrators
Ellis Chappell
Todd Koncsol
Michael Romeo

**Symbols and
Cover Design**
Smart Graphics

Globe Design
Mountain High

Contributing Writers

Margaret Ardwin
Eric Baron
Sandy Buleza
Ana Marie Castle
Betty Ciacchi
Jennifer Copersino
Claire Corcoran
David-Michel Davies

Mark Davies
Susan Dietz
Rulene DiFrancesco
Shelly Fennell
Jacqueline Flamm
Kevin Flynn
Beth Gill

Diane Frenick
Rebecca Greco
Beth Hanson
Arnold Henderson
Lisa Herz
Ethan Klein
Cathy Lemp

Tammy Mendelson
Merrie Snow
Jill Stauffer
Christopher Taranta
Tom Weathers
John Wollerton
Betsy Wooster

School Curriculum Advisory Board

Sandy Buleza
Science Curriculum Specialist
Liberty Science Center
Jersey City, New Jersey

Merrie Snow
Science, Math, Social Studies Curriculum Developer
Scotch Plains-Fanwood Public School District
Scotch Plains, New Jersey

Environmental Advisory Board

Barbara MacGregor
One World Environmental Education Services
Lacy, Washington

David Sousa
Science Consultant
Plainfield, New Jersey

PHOTO CREDITS VOLUME 4

Contents

ACKNOWLEDGMENTS

For providing encouragement and enthusiasm during the initial stages of this work, the editors thank:
Robert F. Geigengack, Director of the Institute of Environment, University of Pennsylvania
Andrew R. McGhie, Laboratory for Research on the Structure of Matter, University of Pennsylvania

For contributing environmental advice and expertise and for granting access to the outstanding materials in their facilities, the editors thank The Academy of Natural Sciences of Philadelphia, especially **Roger L. Thomas** and **Henry P. Stoebenau.**

THE ACADEMY OF NATURAL SCIENCES OF PHILADELPHIA

Founded in 1812, The Academy of Natural Sciences of Philadelphia is the oldest natural science research institution in the Western Hemisphere. From its science research beginnings, the Academy has broadened its activities to include education and exhibitions. The Academy's work is carried out by two research divisions (the Division of Biodiversity and Evolution and the Environmental Research Division [ERD]), the library, and its public museum.

The Division of Biodiversity and Evolution studies the identity, relationships, and ecology of organisms. Through the Academy's extensive biological collections and individual research efforts, Academy scientists explore the diversity of Earth's life-forms and their evolution, adaptation, survival, and extinction. The Environmental Research Division (ERD) pioneered the assessment of water-quality issues and their impact on living resources. One of the largest fresh-water research organizations in the United States, its three principal research centers are organized along a watershed continuum. The centers focus on the effects of land use on streams and rivers; large rivers, wetlands, and lakes; and estuaries, bays and near-coastal waters.

The research divisions join with the Academy museum and library, located in central Philadelphia, to offer a broad range of exhibits and educational programs for families, teachers, students, and concerned citizens.

Preface

The eight volumes of *The Grolier Library of Environmental Concepts and Issues* are organized in broad, readable chapters rather than in the brief entries normally found in encyclopedias. Each volume lets you explore one whole aspect of the world around us, such as air or water or energy. Each chapter treats a whole topic within that aspect—you can sit down and read it through.

Volume 1: Ecosystem Earth

From the fringes of our solar system down to the very center of Earth, forces are shaping the world we live in. These physical forces rule our environment.

Volume 2: Air: The Invisible Resource

Pure, transparent air is actually a mixture of gases sensitive to the effects of human activity. We are learning how to determine when the air quality is bad for us and for other living things. But are we learning quickly enough what to do about it?

Volume 3: Water: A Finite Resource

Water is a remarkable substance, able to dissolve and transport the nutrients plants and animals need, but also able to dissolve and transport the poisons that may kill them. Its quality is fundamental to the health of every ecosystem.

Volume 4: Energy

Energy flows down from the Sun and up from Earth's hot core, warming life from the deep sea to the high mountains. Human transformation of this energy may free the Sun's energy trapped in coal, or turn the energy of underground steam into electricity. Energy cannot be created or destroyed, but its transformation from one form to another makes many things possible, for good or bad.

Volume 5: Living Resources

Plants, animals, and soil work together as a natural system, but also as a system that humans can use to raise food and other products. We call it agriculture. From ancient hunting and gathering to the latest "environmentally friendly" farming techniques, human use of Earth's living resources have had to fit into natural patterns—or risk disaster.

Volume 6: Using the Earth's Resources

Resources from the land include the many ores that provide our metals, but the life-giving soil that lies on top of those ores may be even more essential to human life. At times mining disturbs or pollutes the soil. Our waste disposal makes certain lands unfit for other uses. Our activities in harvesting resources from the land and sea provide opportunities to feed people and raise living standards—if we are careful of the side effects.

Volume 7: The Earth's Ecosystems

Plants and animals do not live in isolation but in groupings called "ecosystems." In an ecosystem, each species depends on others and on nonliving components of that system—soil, water, air, sunlight, and so on. The ways that one part depends on another can be indirect and surprising. Fragile ecosystems can collapse if a very few components change. Yet all across the globe ecosystems do thrive and adapt to change. They support all the varied life of Earth, from equatorial forest to frozen Arctic tundra.

Volume 8: People and the Environment

Clues to ice ages, mass extinctions, and other past changes in Earth's environment have been recorded in rocks and fossils, in the ice of glaciers, and in paintings made by humans on ancient cave walls. We humans have brought environmental changes of our own—and the will to control them. Over the years, many people and organizations have asked the questions we have learned to call "environmental issues." As science provides new technologies, such as genetic engineering, the 21st century will have new means to approach the issues that the 20th century has raised.

An index is at the back of each volume from 1 through 7. Volume 8 draws all of them together. The glossary is at the end of Volume 8.

Our planet's only satellite—The Moon.

Energy and Earth

When compared to other celestial bodies, the Sun is a rather ordinary star. Its effects on the Earth, however, are vital to the continued functioning of the planet. Research shows the Sun to be volatile and dynamic. Its gaseous body is a huge nuclear reactor that produces radiant energy, seen and experienced on the Earth as heat, light, and invisible forms of energy. Emissions from the Sun hit our planet's surface, causing changes in climate, light, and life cycles. Sunspots and solar winds affect the amount and intensity of energy intercepted by the Earth and give us an idea of the tremendous reactions occurring on the Sun's surface. Our eyes see light from the Sun as white, but after entering the Earth's atmosphere, it can be broken down into its constituent colors through prisms and even water droplets in the atmosphere, creating rainbows. The Sun's energy can also produce unexpected phenomena such as mirages by heating the air unevenly so that things seen through it may seem distorted or out of place.

THE SUN'S ENERGY

Relationship Between Sun and Earth. Solar energy is the heat, light, and other forms of radiative energy emitted from the Sun. The Sun is a star, just like the dots of bright lights that make up the constellations. The Sun's energy travels in all directions, providing light and heat in varying amounts around the Solar System. Earth is the third planet from the Sun; its distance from the Sun ranges from 147.25 million kilometers (91.5 million miles) to 152 million kilometers (94.5 million miles), depending on the time of year. At such a great distance, the planet receives only about one billionth of the Sun's energy. If the Earth were any closer to or farther from the Sun, the intensity of heat and light would be quite different, and the planet's unique collection of plant and animal life would have developed in different ways, or perhaps not at all.

What Is the Sun? Throughout history, many theories have been put forth to explain the brilliant energy generated by the Sun. Ancient peoples once attributed the power of the Sun to deities, or gods. These people worshipped the Sun as they would a holy being, believing the Sun god would bring them health, prosperity, and good crops.

As a scientific community began to develop, it became obvious that the Sun was not a deity or an interactive being. As the universe was mapped out,

Seen from space, Earth shows swirling white cloud patterns that are driven by the Sun's heating of the atmosphere.

the discipline of astronomy was born. Most early European astronomers argued that the Sun, other planets, and the stars all orbited Earth. This theory, taught to students for hundreds of years, was eventually disproved by Nicolas Copernicus (1473-1543), a 16th-century Polish astronomer now considered the founder of modern astronomy. Still other astronomers correctly theorized that the Sun could not spread so much heat to us if it was not itself much hotter than

ENVIROBIT

The Sun composes about 99.9% of the dust and gas that made up the forming Solar System. The remaining 0.01% formed all of the planets, their moons, asteroids, comets, and debris.

any temperature generated on Earth; therefore, it would be impossible for the types of chemical and physical reactions that occur on Earth to occur the same way on the Sun. They also recognized that organisms on Earth perceive the Sun as a burning inferno but correctly surmised that if ordinary fire, or combustion, were the source of the Sun's energy, the hot ball would have run out of fuel and oxygen and burned itself out millions of years ago.

Once scientists had learned from Sir Isaac Newton to think in terms of the new concept of gravity, an early explanation for the Sun's hot rays was gravitational attraction, a process exhibited by other stars. This attraction is created when a star's small particles of matter create a gravitational pull upon one another, causing the star to shrink and become more dense. This process would allow a star to produce energy for about 50 million years. This theory was rejected, however, because the Sun is about 4.6 billion years old.

Thermonuclear Reactions. Scientists in the 20th century proposed the most likely theory behind the Sun's energy—thermonuclear reactions. Many questions about the Sun went unanswered until scientists discovered that the Sun's energy-production mechanism is actually a type of nuclear reaction. In 1905,

German physicist Albert Einstein (1879-1955) proposed that through nuclear reactions, a small amount of mass could be converted to a large amount of energy. Scientists then raced to find the materials and exact methods for the production of that energy. It has since been generally agreed that the Sun's core is composed of enough tightly packed atomic nuclei and electrons to provide fuel for billions of years. By the middle of the 20th century, it was known that the Sun's deep temperature is about 15,000,000 Kelvin (about 15,000,000°C, or 27,000,000°F). With this tremendous amount of heat, the nuclei within the Sun can collide and combine into new, heavier nuclei in a fusion reaction.

The nuclei that are converted begin as pairs of hydrogen (H) nuclei. After fusion, they become helium (He). During fusion reactions, the Sun consumes 598 million metric tons (657 million tons) of hydrogen nuclei and converts them to 593.8 million metric tons (652.5 million tons) of helium nuclei. Therefore, the 4.1 million metric tons (4.5 million tons) lost to the fusion process is the quantity converted directly to energy. The heat and light experienced on Earth are the products of the release of this massive amount of energy. (See Chapter 7 for a detailed description of fusion.)

THE SUN'S MAKEUP

The Photosphere. The "surface" of the Sun is called the *photosphere*, which means "sphere of light." It is not, however, a solid surface but a layer of hot and glowing gases that we may think of as a surface simply because we cannot see beyond it. The photosphere's temperature is between 7,500 Kelvin (7,227°C, or 13,040°F) at its base to 4,700 Kelvin (4,427°C, or 8,000°F) at its top. Scientists have noted that the photosphere has a recognizable texture resembling bright granules separated by dark areas that look like the strands of a spider web. One theory is that the grains are the tops of plumes of gas that rise and fall through the photosphere. Continually forming and disappearing, they are hundreds of kilometers (miles) in diameter.

Sunspots. Sunspots appear as dark spots on the Sun's photosphere; they appear dark because they

 **ENVIROBIT**

About 4.5 billion years ago, the Earth's atmosphere was composed of components that no form of life could withstand—water, hydrogen cyanide, ammonia, methane, sulfur, iodine, bromine, and chlorine. Because of the influence of the Sun on the molecules of this early atmosphere and the oxygen added to it by early plants, the air we breathe today is made up of 78% nitrogen, 21% oxygen, and tiny amounts of carbon dioxide and several other gases.

are much cooler than the surrounding photosphere. Caused by magnetic storms in the photosphere, sunspots can measure 10,000 to 50,000 kilometers (6,200 to 31,100 miles). The largest sunspot on record grew as large as 160,000 kilometers (100,000 miles) in diameter, more than 12 times the diameter of the Earth. A sunspot begins as what looks like a dark pinhole, called a pore, which multiplies into several pores that eventually form a large spot on the photosphere. Sunspots usually have an umbra, a dark, circular center that is much cooler than the rest of the photosphere. A lighter area called the penumbra surrounds it and is caused by rays that shoot out from the center of the umbra.

Sunspots have fascinated astronomers since they were first noticed about 400 years ago. Galileo Galilei (1564-1642) was the first scientist to notice that sunspots drift around the Sun's surface. It was eventually learned that the Sun is a gaseous body, and that the sunspots are not fixed to one location. Since that time, much has been learned about these odd phenomena. Sunspots form and disappear in cycles of about 11 years but have been known to last anywhere from 7 to 17 years. They appear in only two sections of the Sun—between latitudes 40 degrees and 5 degrees of the Northern and Southern hemispheres. When newly formed, a few spots will appear near the 35 degree latitude mark. About 5 years later, the spots will reach a growth peak and begin to move toward the Sun's equator. Over the next 6 years, the sunspots slowly

decrease in number but continue their journey toward the equator. When they reach their destination, the spots disappear and a new cycle of sunspot growth begins. George E. Hale (1868-1938), a U.S. astronomer, was the first to theorize that sunspots mark the north and south poles of a magnetic field and that from one 11-year cycle to the next, these magnetic poles reverse positions, creating a 22-year magnetic cycle on the Sun's surface.

 ENVIROBIT

- Studies conducted in 1991 showed evidence that quick cycles of sunspots correspond with warmer climates on Earth, and that slow sunspot cycles bring colder weather. Moreover, during the past 100 years, sunspot cycles have declined from 11.7 years to 9.7 years, and the Earth's surface temperature has increased 0.6°C (1.08°F).
- More than 200 sunspots were recorded during a peak period in 1990.

Chromosphere. Above the photosphere is the *chromosphere*, which means "sphere of color." The chromosphere can be seen from Earth during total solar eclipses, when the bright central disk is blocked out by the Moon. Then the chromosphere appears to the human eye as a reddish outline of the Sun. In the chromosphere, plages, bright flashes of light, appear over sunspots. Other phenomena that occur in the chromosphere are solar flares, which look like volcanic eruptions from the Sun's surface. The flares are actually emissions of high-energy radiation, such as X-rays and radio waves, and charged particles. Other action in the chromosphere involves *prominences*, a term coined by early astronomers to describe the masses of gas that surround the Sun during an eclipse. Today, there are several theoretical categories of prominences. One is a quiescent prominence, a flare that can retain its shape for months at a time, or disappear quite quickly. Other prominences can extend more than 161,000 kilometers (100,000

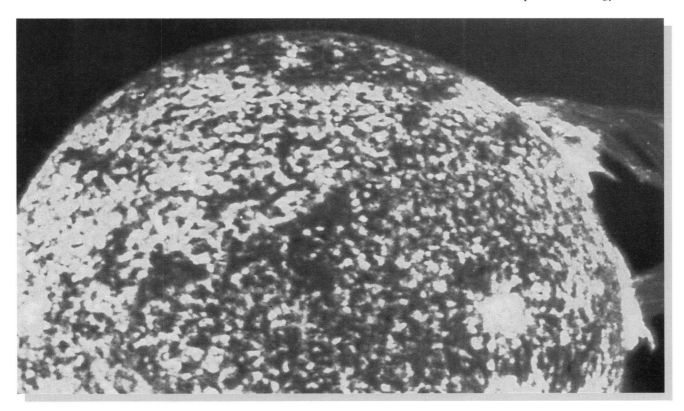

In filtered light, the Sun's mottled surface can be seen. To the upper right, a large solar flare arcs outward from the surface.

miles) and can be several thousand kilometers wide. Prominences can look like rain falling from the corona into the chromosphere or can take the shape of a burst of matter, moving outward from the Sun at 1,609 kilometers (1,000 miles) per second.

Corona. The corona is the outer atmosphere of the Sun; its faint glow is overwhelmed by the light of the bright photosphere below. Because it is usually invisible to researchers on Earth, opportunities to study the corona had been limited to periods of eclipse, when it appears as a luminous halo around the Sun. Today, it can be studied using a machine called a coronagraph, which artificially blocks light from the Sun's central disc much as the Moon blocks it in a natural eclipse. The corona usually emits streamers, long flashes of light. When few sunspots are present on the photosphere, the corona has very long streamers along the Sun's equator, with shorter rays at the poles. When the magnetic poles of the sunspots shift, the shape of the corona also changes, forming a circle of sorts. It was once thought to be

made of coronium (an imaginary element not found on Earth) emissions. Later, atomic analysis of the

ENVIROBIT

A study presented in 1994 suggests that in 1.1 billion years, the Sun will be 10% more luminous than it is now, which will lead to a catastrophic greenhouse effect. The study further predicts that in 7.8 billion years, the Sun will have expanded to 170 times its current diameter, and will engulf Mercury, the innermost planet. It will then shrink down over a period of about 120 million years. At the same time, its gravitational grip will shrink, and the Earth, heated by the Sun to become a red-hot molten rock, will move away from the Sun and, therefore, will not be destroyed by the intense heat. The Sun will then eject its outer portions and become a white dwarf, a dim and shrunken star.

During a total solar eclipse, the chromosphere is seen as a "halo" around the Sun.

corona's spectrum showed that its lines are produced when iron (Fe), nickel (Ni), and calcium (Ca) gases have a low density and combine at a high temperature. Research has shown that the corona is

ENVIROBIT

In 1989, powerful geomagnetic storms triggered by solar activity caused vision problems for astronauts in the space shuttle *Atlantis*, disrupted power systems and radio communications on Earth, and disturbed the operation of satellites that depend on the Earth's magnetic field for orientation.

made of plasma, an extremely hot gas made up of charged negative and positive ions that have been supercompressed into a phase past the gaseous stage. Plasma, unlike a regular gas, conducts electric-

ity and can be affected by magnetic fields. The temperature of the corona is about 2,000,000 Kelvin (2,000,000°C, or 3,600,000°F), but the corona does not provide the Solar System with nearly as much radiation as is emitted from the core of the Sun.

THE EARTH'S MAGNETISM AND SOLAR WINDS

Earth's Magnetic Field. The Earth is surrounded by a magnetic field. Thought to have been created by the influence of the Sun's magnetic field, it appeared billions of years ago when the Earth itself was forming from a swirling ball of gas and dust. Electrically conductive material in the dust cloud was influenced by the Sun's magnetism, creating an electric current in the process. This electric current formed an invisible field around the newly formed planet and is the shield that protects us from solar winds. Without the protective magnetic field, life on Earth would not exist.

Solar Winds. Solar winds stream from the Sun at

The tail of a comet points away from the Sun, no matter what direction the comet itself is traveling.

The beautiful lights of the aurora australis are common near the South Pole.

about 50 million kilometers (31 million miles) per day. Composed of the electrons, protons, and alpha radiation in plasma clouds, they reach the Earth about three days after leaving the Sun. Solar winds can travel as much as 50 times the distance between the Sun and the Earth, reaching far beyond the Solar System. The solar wind's particles are emitted by the corona and flow past the Sun's gravitational field, taking with them some of the magnetic particles generated within the Sun. Because of the rotation of the Sun and the steady emission of these charged particles, the solar wind carves curves into space and can deflect the tails of passing comets away from the Sun. Although the Earth's magnetosphere deflects solar winds, the upper layers of the atmosphere can be somewhat affected. One such effect is a magnetic storm, which can produce severe weather conditions, radio transmission disruption, and polar auroras on the Earth. (See Volume 1, Chapter 1, for more information on solar winds.)

Auroras. Auroras are some of the most beautiful natural effects of the Earth-Sun interface. About 80 to 480 kilometers (50 to 300 miles) above the Earth's poles, atoms and molecules in the ionosphere become ionized, or electrically charged, and excited by the solar wind. As the atoms return to their normal energy states, they release electromagnetic energy in the form of visible light, causing expanses of bright lights to appear in the sky. Depending on which atoms become ionized, different hues, such as purple and green, can be produced. When this occurs near the North Pole, it is referred to as the aurora borealis; near the South Pole, it is known as the aurora australis.

Reversal of the Magnetic Poles. Many scientists agree that Earth's magnetic field has been weakening for the past 2,000 years and may temporarily disappear in another 2,000 years. This is part of a natural cycle that occurs when the magnetic field reverses. The magnetic poles are not the geographic North and South poles seen on a map. The Earth's magnetic poles are created by magnetic interaction at the center of the planet. Earth's iron and nickel inner core is solid in the center and surrounded by a

molten, or liquid, outer core. The temperature at the center of the Earth is about 4,980°C (9,000°F). It is theorized that the combination of uneven, intense heat and the composition of the core produces convection currents, or circular waves, in the liquid outer core. The convection currents create, throughout the Earth, magnetic fields which interact with the magnetic fields of the Sun and Moon.

On the Earth, the force of magnetism is evidenced in newly created rocks as well as in rock formations that are billions of years old. Rocks containing iron-rich materials known as magnetite and titanomagnetite are easily magnetized. When a rock is formed, such as through cooling and hardening of magma after a volcanic eruption, the microscopic crystals of these minerals can build into their structure the magnetic polarity of Earth's magnetic field at that particular time when they were cooling. By studying the magnetic blueprints of rocks of different time periods, scientists can pinpoint the changing location of the magnetic poles throughout the Earth's geologic history.

ENERGY'S ENTRANCE TO THE EARTH'S SYSTEMS

As solar radiation hits the Earth, it is intercepted by the atmosphere and either reflected back into space or absorbed by greenhouse gases and other materials. About 480 kilometers (300 miles) above the Earth's surface is the thermopause, the outer boundary of the atmosphere. As the first zone to intercept sunlight, the thermosphere is where intercepted solar radiation becomes insolation, the energy that hits and enters the Earth's atmosphere. Insolation at the thermopause is called the solar constant. The amount of energy produced at this point is 1.94 calories per square centimeter per minute. A calorie is the amount of energy it takes to heat 1 gram of water by 1° Celsius (1.8° Fahrenheit). The Earth's systems have developed around this amount of energy. Any change in the amount of solar radiation that hits the Earth could have dramatic results. From 1980 to 1989, scientists used test data from a satellite called the Solar Maximum Mission, or Solar Max, to measure the amount of energy released by the Sun. The data showed that the solar constant was relatively stable, with variations of only 0.04%. During sunspot activity, the largest change was measured at 0.3%.

Because the Earth is more or less spherical in shape, the Sun's energy is unevenly distributed over the rounded surface. Depending on a location's angle in relation to the position of the Sun, some places, such as those at high altitudes, receive a glancing and less intense sunlight than other places, such as those along the equator, where the light strikes the surface more squarely. This difference in energy distribution energizes the biosphere and is the main factor behind the motion of the atmosphere and the oceans.

Insolation is measured around the world and from outside Earth's orbit. Weather patterns, important indicators of the Sun's effect on the planet, are mapped by satellites, such as the U.S. Landsat satellites, the French SPOT spacecraft, and the former-Soviet Kosmos series spacecraft, which show a variety of visible and infrared data regarding a particular location. With further research on weather and temperature data, the patterns and influences of the Sun's energy upon the Earth's systems will become more apparent.

LIGHT AND HEAT

Composition of Light. Energy from the Sun is transmitted to the Earth in many forms. Radiant energy is composed of 8% ultraviolet, X-ray, and gamma rays; 47% visible light; and 45% infrared light. Organisms on Earth have evolved to have eyes that respond to varying degrees of light and colors. Different skin types and tones are also a part of evolution. The skin of animals such as chameleons changes color to match the light reflecting off different surfaces. Color is created when a beam of white light hits an object, causing the atoms of the object to reflect some wavelengths of light, while others are absorbed and go unseen. For example, red objects are those that reflect red light to our eyes.

Color of the Sky. The sky is not an object in the same way a red book is, but it, too, shows colors. The sky changes colors several times during a 24-hour period. At dawn and sunset, the sky is reddish, while during the day it is usually blue. Such changes are regulated by air molecules, airborne dust molecules, and water vapor that reflect and refract, or scatter, the wavelengths of light. This process is also called diffusion. During the periods of sunrise and sunset, sunlight reaches the Earth through the dust-laden air near Earth's surface. The Sun's light is reflected by large dust particles that scatter long wavelengths (red end of the spectrum) throughout the atmosphere, producing a red sky. During the day, air molecules scatter short wavelengths (blue end of the spectrum), producing a blue sky. On a foggy day, the sky appears white because cloud droplets are of a larger diameter than light wavelengths, and all the colors of the spectrum are scattered equally, producing no distinguishing color. Furthermore, outer space appears black because there is no atmosphere to scatter the light waves.

Mirages and Illusions. Humans have been mystified through the ages by "tricks of light." Throughout history, desert people, sailors, and others have noted the strange occurrences of mirages, optical illusions that trick the eye into seeing reflected images of distant objects. A mirage is created when light rays are bent, or refracted, by the atmosphere, which is always heavy and dense at the Earth's surface, and rarefied, or less dense, farther from the surface. The difference in air density makes the atmosphere act as a large wide-bottomed prism that bends all incoming light rays downward. If the effect is particularly intense, the result is called a looming mirage. An example of a looming mirage occurs in Chicago, where people can sometimes see the opposite shore of Lake Michigan, though it is so far off as

ENVIROBIT

In 1818, a polar mirage of a huge mountain chain at the entrance to the Northwest Passage caused British explorer Captain John Ross (1777-1856) to end his search for a passage to China.

A miragelike effect causes the setting Sun to remain visible in the sky for a short time after it has actually set behind the horizon. Its light is bent by the thick layer of air we are looking through, making the Sun appear higher in the sky than it actually is and stay visible longer.

to be below the horizon and out of the line of human sight even on the clearest days.

There are two types of mirages—superior and inferior. Superior mirages are caused by layers of cool, dense air layered over warmer air. The warm air bends, or refracts, light rays, which create an upside-down image that seems to hover over the actual object. A classic superior mirage is that of an upside-down ship hovering over an actual ship as it moves through the water. In some cases, several copies of the object may appear floating above. Inferior mirages are much more common and are typically seen on summer days behind cars traveling over hot, flat roads. In this case, hot rarefied air lies in a thin layer over a road. A car traveling through this air refracts light rays upward, and a shimmering reflection of the sky is projected behind the car.

A combination of inferior and superior mirages intensified by looming produces the famous Fata Morgana. Named for the fabled sorceress Morgan le Fay, sister of King Arthur of Britain, the Fata Morgana appears as shape-shifting castles hovering over the Strait of Messina between Italy and Sicily. In reality, light rays bent by shifting layers of air reflect the homes built on cliffs across the Strait thus forming the mirage.

Sources

Calder, Nigel. "A Globe Warmed By Sunspots?" *World Press Review* 41 (July 1994).

Christopherson, Robert W. *Geosystems.* New York: Macmillan Publishing Co., 1992.

"Devastating Solar Activity in 1989," *Sky and Telescope,* 79 (June 1990).

Ludlum, David M. "Rainbows," *Country Journal* 15 (July 1988).

Mayor, Adrienne. "Marine Mirages," *Sea Frontiers* 34 (February 1988).

Rees, Robin, senior executive ed. *The Way Nature Works.* New York: Macmillan Publishing Co., 1992. © Mitchell Beazley International Ltd.

"The Fate of the Sun," *Sky and Telescope* 87 (May 1994).

CHAPTER TWO

Energy in the Environment

Earth's millions of species have evolved within the comfortable global temperatures created by the Sun. Through the greenhouse effect and photosynthesis, sunlight is responsible for the growth of plants, which in turn help maintain the atmosphere. In recent years, a theory known as global warming has caused scientists to evaluate the impact human-made emissions of carbon dioxide (CO_2) and other greenhouse gases may have on the atmosphere. Global warming and another modern dilemma, the depletion of the ozone layer high in the atmosphere, may be linked to increased emissions from industrial sources. Because of holes in the ozone layer, humans are warned to protect themselves from harmful emissions that are entering Earth's systems. Ultraviolet (UV) light, along with other forms of high-energy radiation, are able to penetrate down to the Earth's surface, disrupting the genetic makeup of humans and other organisms and creating a frightening scenario that has become the focus of intense study.

THE BALANCE OF ENERGY IN THE ENVIRONMENT

Earth receives energy externally from the Sun, as well as tiny amounts from distant stars and other celestial bodies. Internally, Earth produces heat from its core. But at a temperature rise of only 25°C (77°F) per kilometer of descent, this interior heat is hardly enough to maintain the planet's ecosystems. Consequently, it is the Sun that is Earth's main source of energy.

The atmosphere and the surface of the planet are heated unevenly due to seasonal fluctuations and the fact that the Sun's rays hit different points on Earth's curvature in varying intensities. The energy received comes in shortwave radiation, which is composed of ultraviolet light, visible light, near-infrared wavelengths, and longwave radiation, or heat waves. The movement of these waves through the air and water is known as transmission. Much of the energy hitting the atmosphere is immediately reflected back into space. Energy entering Earth's systems is trapped by land, water, clouds, and greenhouse gases and is retained inside the biosphere until it is eventually radiated back into space.

Seasons. Solar energy enters Earth's atmosphere and warms it unevenly. As warmer air masses tend to expand and rise, cooler ones tend to contract and sink, forming turbulence, or patterns of air currents.

Light and heat energy in the atmosphere make Earth look like a glowing sphere, even from distant space.

This incoming energy drives almost all the planet's atmospheric variations, including storms, winds, and water currents. This energy is known as insolation. Because of changes in insolation, the world experiences varying weather patterns throughout the year. During winter, for example, the Northern Hemisphere is tipped away from the Sun and receives much less solar energy than in the summer; therefore, insolation during winter is decreased. With less insolation, a location experiences colder temperatures.

Reflection, Refraction, and Absorption. About half the radiant energy hitting Earth's atmosphere is either reflected or absorbed by the upper atmosphere and never reaches Earth's surface. The visible and ultraviolet energy reflected off the thermosphere, the outer layer of the atmosphere, is called reflection. Albedo, the measurement of the reflective quality of a surface, helps determine which light waves will enter Earth's atmosphere. Dark-colored surfaces have a low albedo, whereas light-colored surfaces have a high albedo. For example, a white sheet of paper reflects light well, whereas a black piece of paper does not reflect much light but instead absorbs it and changes it to heat. Smooth surfaces increase the level of albedo;

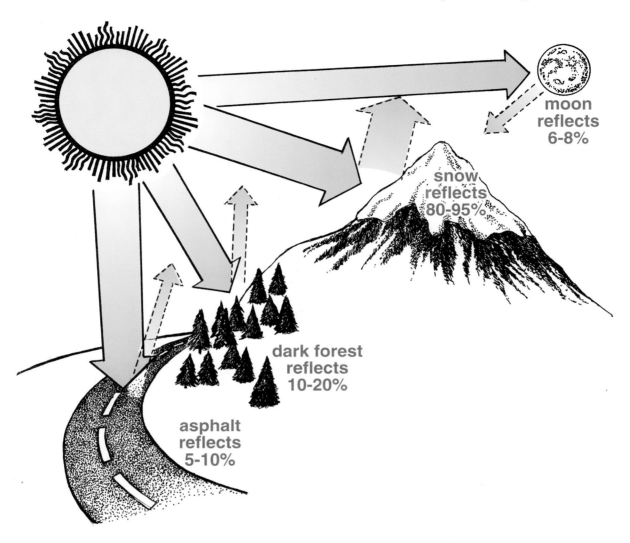

Different surfaces, such as dark forests or white ice, reflect different percentages of the sunlight that strikes them. The percentage reflected is called the albedo of that kind of surface.

rough surfaces reduce it. Over a one-year period, Earth and the atmosphere reflect about 31% of insolation entering the planet's systems. Of this, clouds reflect about 21%; continental masses and bodies of water reflect 3%; and the atmosphere reflects the remaining 7%. From space, Earth looks like a glowing, lively place. This is because the amount of light continually reflecting off its surface into space makes the planet shine.

The absorption of radiant energy occurs when molecules in the atmosphere absorb and convert energy from one form to another. Direct and diffused light that has not been reflected from the Earth's surface is absorbed by it and converted into infrared radiation, or heat, or is taken in by plants for use in photosynthesis. Molecules that have absorbed the energy become excited, causing them to radiate more energy, thereby creating a rise in temperature.

As light enters the atmosphere, it is scattered by gases, dust particles, cloud droplets, ice, and water vapor, altering its transmission path. This is why the sky appears blue and sunsets red. The short wavelengths of visible light are blues and violets. When they hit small gas molecules in the air, they are scattered the most and make the lower atmosphere appear blue. At sunset, insolation passes through a thicker mass of atmosphere at a different angle, allowing the long wavelengths of visible light, the red light waves, to dominate the horizon.

Insolation is also refracted, meaning that as light passes through space and enters the atmosphere, it becomes bent. Refraction is important to Earth's energy systems because it actually extends the amount of daylight by eight minutes every day. A refracted image of the Sun is delivered from space through the atmosphere. Thus, when we watch the Sun rise, we see a refracted image of the Sun rising past the horizon about four minutes before the Sun actually rises. At sunset, the Sun actually sets about four minutes after we see it fall below the horizon, but its image is refracted through the atmosphere, making it appear as if it is setting. Because of this, scientists cannot predict the exact time of sunrise or sunset within these four-minute refraction periods.

ENVIROBIT

In 1990, a joint U.S.–Soviet research team discovered a community of sponges, bacterial mats, snails, fish, and transparent shrimp living in a hydrothermal vent community, a spring of heated water, at the bottom of Siberia's 25-million-year-old Lake Baikal, the oldest and deepest lake on Earth. Scientists believe these organisms rely on chemosynthesis, energy made from chemical sources, rather than photosynthesis, to obtain energy.

PHOTOSYNTHESIS

Nearly all Earth's inhabitants rely on solar radiation for food, warmth, light, and energy. Through-

Plants, even underwater, absorb light energy from the Sun and release oxygen as a by-product.

out the planet's history, its proximity to the Sun has been the most influential factor in the growth and development of life cycles, the creation of the atmosphere, and the generation of energy. Many scientists believe that millions of years ago, organic life-forms began to exploit the Sun's rays as energy and food. Simple plants, such as mosses and lichens, were some of the first organisms to use light energy as food. Scientists believe that about 3 billion years ago, even more primitive plants, such as cyanobacteria, filled the oceans. These first plants used photosynthetic reactions in the same way modern plants do. Without the Sun's influence on these early life-forms, the rudimentary building blocks of life on Earth would not have evolved. Fossil fuels also developed

from the decay and compression of these early plants. Energy absorbed from the Sun was stored in the plants' cells. Millions of years later, the burning of fossil fuels releases that stored energy.

Plants still play a vital role in harnessing the Sun's energy. Through the process of photosynthesis, plants absorb photons, or particles of light, from sunshine and convert them to chemical energy that can be used to make food. Because nearly all living organisms on Earth rely on photosynthesis directly or indirectly, it is considered one of the most important reactions of the Sun–Earth interface.

Photosynthesis is reliant on chlorophyll, the green pigment in plants. Chlorophyll pigments in a plant's leaves absorb different-colored wavelengths of light

The natural greenhouse effect has helped keep the planet warm for millions of years. Various gases in the atmosphere trap some of the heat that Earth would otherwise radiate out to space, just as florists can use glass greenhouses to keep plants warm.

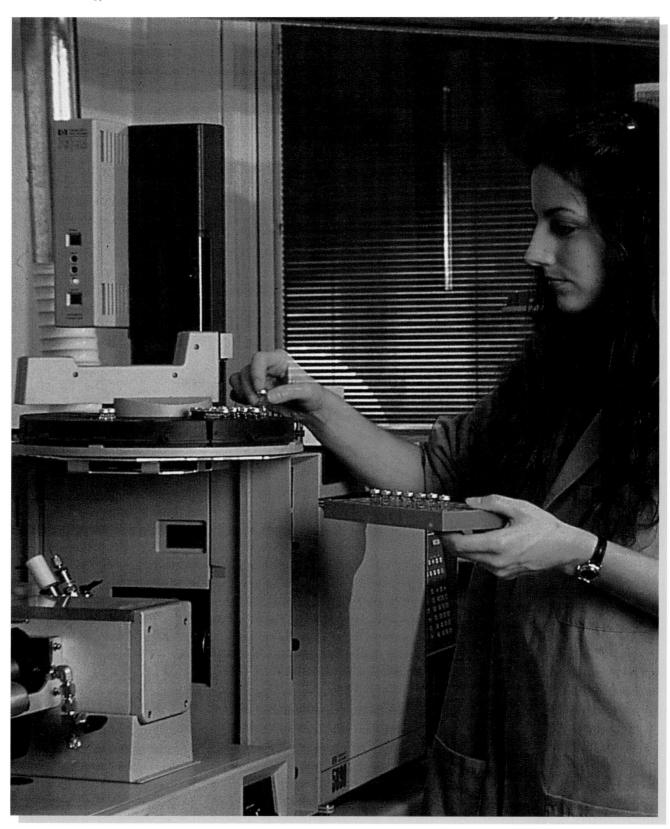

A mass spectrometer can detect the various materials in a mixture, such as a sample of atmosphere containing traces of various greenhouse gases.

energy. Pigments of various colors exist in many plants. A form of chlorophyll called phycocyanin, for example, gives blue-green algae their characteristic color. Chlorophyll transforms light waves into chemical energy, which is then used by the plant to grow and carry on its normal processes.

Early plant life used the Sun's energy to create our modern atmosphere. When Earth was formed, its atmosphere was composed of substances that would kill all modern life on the planet. But huge quantities of carbon dioxide and other greenhouse gases began to trap heat from the Sun. This warmed Earth to the point at which it could sustain life. Photosynthesis allowed plants to take in carbon dioxide gas, thereby reducing the vast quantities of the gas in the atmosphere, and produce oxygen molecules as a by-product. In such a way, photosynthetic reactions are responsible for our modern atmosphere.

The Sun and the Greenhouse Effect

Earth receives a tremendous amount of energy from the Sun, about half of which makes its way through the outer layers of the atmosphere to eventually hit the planet's surface. Molecules of oxygen (O_2) and ozone (O_3) in the outer atmosphere are the primary agents that reflect harmful ultraviolet radiation back into space. Energy that enters the system is generally composed of visible and infrared (heat) light waves. The radiation is absorbed by the land and oceans, explaining why Earth's average temperature is about 15°C (59°F), while temperatures in outer space are recorded at -270°C (-454°F).

Light is also reradiated back into space in infrared wavelengths. The amount of light reradiated is about twice the amount that enters Earth's atmosphere. With this ratio and with no means of trapping the energy, Earth would soon freeze over. However, greenhouse gases, such as carbon dioxide (CO_2), methane (CH_4), and water vapor (H_2O), trap and absorb the infrared radiation and return about 84% of the energy that Earth reradiates back down to the surface and the atmosphere. The gases are composed of invisible molecules that absorb energy in the infrared region of the electromagnetic spectrum.

The molecules absorb energy and begin to vibrate. The amount of absorption of infrared light can be measured with an infrared spectrometer.

In the atmosphere, greenhouse gases absorb infrared energy, vibrate for some time, and then return to their normal, unexcited state. Any molecule that vibrates when infrared energy is absorbed is a potential greenhouse gas. Chlorofluorocarbons (CFCs) are an example of substances that can absorb and retain heat. As the name implies, chlorofluorocarbons are composed of chlorine (Cl), fluorine (F), and carbon (C). CFCs do not occur in nature but are industrially produced compounds used as propellants in aerosol sprays, sterilizers in hospitals, and solvents that break down oil and grease. CFCs were first created by the DuPont Corporation in the 1950s for use in refrigeration systems. They replaced the extremely hazardous ammonia (NH_3) and sulfur dioxide (SO_2) solutions previously used in such systems, and were perceived as an achievement for the chemical industry as well as a boon for consumer health and welfare. As released CFCs drifted up through the atmosphere, however, they came to react with other molecules already there and began to cause problems. Today, CFCs are in the process of being banned by most nations because of their theorized contribution to increased global warming.

Rising Levels of Greenhouse Gases. Today, there is great concern regarding a rise in the atmospheric levels of greenhouse gases. Earth was originally made habitable by the ability of greenhouse gases to retain heat within the atmosphere; still today natural

Envirobit

In 1994, one study found that certain species of termites, millipedes, cockroaches, and scarab beetles produce a combined output of 10 trillion to 300 trillion grams (352.7 billion ounces to 10.6 trillion ounces) of atmospheric methane released into the atmosphere every year.

sources such as volcanos or decaying vegetation continue to release greenhouse gases. Increases in certain gaseous emissions since the Industrial Revolution, however, have sparked concern among scientists regarding global warming. The combustion of fossil fuels by industries and automobiles has led to increased emissions of carbon dioxide, a major greenhouse gas. Some believe the increased greenhouse gases could retain enough heat to create environmental disasters, such as the melting of polar ice caps and major changes in weather patterns. Data from ice-core samples, which contain air samples from the compaction of snowfalls from more than 160,000 years ago, show that as carbon dioxide levels in the atmosphere rose, temperatures also increased. These samples show that during the Ice Age, the average temperature of the Earth was about 9°C (16.2°F) below the average temperature of the years 1950-1980. They also show that the temperature about 130,000 years ago was just over 16°C (61°F), which is higher than today's average global temperature of 15°C (59°F).

Other researchers consider the greenhouse-gas dilemma far less worrying. They note that global carbon dioxide levels have in the past gone through many cycles of rising and falling. They refer to the same ice-core samples as proof that periods of warming and cooling have always occurred in natural cycles, even before the Industrial Revolution. Many factors may be involved. Natural changes in Earth's orbit affect the distance of the Earth from the Sun and, thus, the angle and intensity at which lightwaves strike the planet. It can be difficult to take so many factors into consideration at once, but many researchers agree that increased industrial emissions do have some effect on increasing the amount of radiation held within the Earth's atmosphere and that the combination of orbital and terrestrial factors may be increasing the global average temperature.

THE SUN AND GLOBAL WARMING AND COOLING

The combination of sunlight and greenhouse gases has given Earth a unique atmosphere and surface capable of supporting a variety of organisms and life. Through the heat-retaining qualities of greenhouse gases (mainly carbon dioxide, methane, and water vapor), Earth is kept at an average global temperature of 15°C (59°F). Throughout history, fluctuations in average temperatures have given rise to periods of ice ages and thawing. Without the greenhouse effect, Earth's average global temperature would be about -18°C (0°F), and the oceans would freeze over.

Global Warming Dilemma. Today, there is much conjecture within the scientific community regarding the increase of industrially emitted greenhouse gases. Even if we observe a rise in temperature, we must then try to estimate what, if any, part of it is due to the action of greenhouse gases in the atmosphere. Many believe an increase in greenhouse gases over the last decades is already trapping significantly more of the Sun's infrared energy that is reradiated from the Earth's surface. Others claim that whatever temperature rise can be observed is only part of a cyclical phenomenon and that industrial and automobile emissions are not affecting this natural cycle.

Global warming was first predicted by Svante Arrhenius (1859-1927), a Swedish chemist who in 1900 theorized that if atmospheric carbon dioxide levels were to double, Earth would experience an increase of 5° to 6°C (9° to 10.8°F) in the global average temperature. Since then, atmospheric carbon dioxide levels have risen by 25%, and global temperatures have increased by 0.5° and 0.7°C (0.9° to 10.3°F). Many scientists point to increased greenhouse emissions as the cause for the warming trend; others see it simply as a natural event. Whatever the reason, global temperatures appear to be rising. This phenomenon is known as global warming.

Global warming relies on the maintenance of Earth's energy balance and the reactions of infrared energy with greenhouse gases. For millennia, Earth's atmospheric radiation system has maintained a relatively steady equilibrium. Because of reflection from Earth's albedo, combined with the absorption of energy by clouds, gases, and dust, only

The Amazon rain forest is just one area of vegetation that absorbs carbon dioxide from the air, reducing levels of this greenhouse gas in the atmosphere.

half of the incoming solar radiation reaches the Earth's surface. Over time, Earth reradiates about 69% of the absorbed radiation into space. The increase in greenhouse gases, whether produced by natural cycles or enhanced by industrial emissions, is causing Earth's energy system to trap large quantities of heat within the atmosphere. Many researchers are concerned with the possible negative consequence to the environment associated with global warming—the melting of the polar ice caps, a rise in sea level, changes in global weather patterns, and changes in the growth of vegetation.

Global Cooling. Global warming may have been temporarily halted by global cooling caused by airborne particles that float in the stratosphere and interfere with the normal reflection and refraction of light waves. In 1982, the eruption of the El Chichón volcano in southern Mexico released a cloud of sulfuric acid (H_2SO_4) and ash about 25 kilometers (15.5 miles) into the sky. This cloud spread out, encircling the entire globe within 21 days. The cloud increased the albedo of the Earth and lowered the global average temperature by 0.5°C (0.9°F). It has been suggested that increased industrial and natural emissions send enough light-blocking particles into the upper atmosphere to offset greenhouse-gas activity, thereby slowing global warming.

Nuclear Winter. We know that large quantities of upper-atmospheric dust can block sunlight, whether the particles are moved aloft by volcanos, winds, or nuclear explosions. This is the nuclear-winter hypothesis: that a nuclear war could so cloud the upper atmosphere with dust as to create a sustained winterlike drop in temperature at the Earth's surface. Paul Crutzen of the Max Planck Institute of West Germany and John Birks of the University of Colorado suggest that if global warming increased to the point where it became out of control, the cooling effect of high-altitude dust could be triggered deliberately by humans to cool Earth down again. The detonation of a series of small nuclear bombs could send enough smoke and particulate matter into the atmosphere to drop the global average temperature by at least 25°C (45°F). This suggestion has been met with much criticism, since the effects of so many deliberate nuclear explosions would affect many ecological and biological systems as well.

THE SUN AND THE OZONE LAYER

The Sun emits many forms of energy—heat, visible light, and invisible light. One form of invisible light is ultraviolet light, which has been found to cause cancer and cataracts in humans. The ozonosphere, commonly known as the ozone layer, lies in the stratosphere, 20 to 50 kilometers (12.4 to 31 miles) above Earth's surface. It is composed of ozone, a highly reactive oxygen molecule composed of three—not two—atoms of oxygen. This ozone (O_3) absorbs ultraviolet light and converts it to infrared energy. Ozone, therefore, filters out harmful UV rays before they can hit Earth's surface.

The ozone layer is not one dense layer, but a band of varying thickness throughout the stratosphere. This sheath has protected Earth from UV rays for the past 500 million years. It has been theorized that since World War II, anthropogenic, or human-caused,

pollutants have altered the balance of the ozone layer, presumably causing it to dissipate at an alarming rate.

The notion of an ozone hole was first suggested in 1974 by F. Sherwood Rowland and Mario J. Molina, two professors at the University of California. They claimed that the manufacturing of chlorofluorocarbons for industrial use was somehow depleting Earth's ozone layer. The professors suggested that CFC molecules were reacting with ozone molecules, transforming them into simple oxygen molecules. Although CFCs are chemically inert at the Earth's surface, ultraviolet light in the stratosphere can split CFC molecules and release their chlorine atoms. The chlorine acts as a catalyst to break stratospheric ozone molecules into normal oxygen molecules. Rowland and Molina predicted that stratospheric ozone would decrease anywhere from 7% to 13% from 1974 to 2074. This theory, however, could not be proven without fuller exploration of the upper atmosphere. It was not until 15 years later that action was taken to reduce CFC production.

Early Signs of Ozone Reduction. Beginning in the early 1970s, atmospheric tests suggested that the ozone layer was, in fact, disappearing. By 1991, scientists recorded an ozone loss of 6%, which was much higher than Rowland's and Molina's initial predictions. Scientists are now trying to find an answer to the stratospheric ozone dilemma. They began with measurements of an ozone hole over Antarctica. Since 1970, tests have shown that the hole has gotten bigger every year and is largest during the early Antarctic spring, which falls in October. The studies found that frozen chlorine emissions are carried by air currents and concentrate over Antarctica, where they thaw during the spring and damage the ozone layer by reacting with ozone molecules. In 1990, the ozone hole covered an area about twice the size of the Antarctic continent. Scientists researching the hole complained of unexpected skin burns from ultraviolet radiation that was not being filtered by the ozone layer.

How Ozone Disappears. Scientists have found that from June to August, CFCs and other ozone-

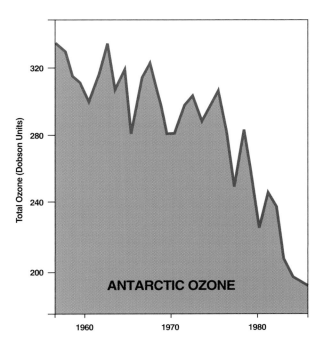

The amount of protective ozone in the atmosphere over Antarctica in October has been declining for more than three decades. (Source of data: British Antarctic Survey at Halley Bay.)

depleting compounds become trapped in ice crystals in the atmosphere over the Antarctic. Beginning in August, the hole begins to form. In October, the ozone layer is damaged when the sunshine melts the ice crystals, releasing the chlorine that transforms the ozone (O_3) into simple oxygen molecules (O_2) and oxygen atoms (O). After two to three months, the air mass containing the chlorine begins to disperse around the world. By early December, the hole is gone. It has also been noted that the chlorine

One study states that the decline in the world's frog population may be due to the thinning of the ozone layer. For the past 200 million years, frogs have lived all over the world. With a reduction in the ozone layer, ultraviolet-B (UVB) rays are allowed to reach the Earth's surface, killing the frog eggs.

atoms can stay active from 40 to 100 years, presenting serious implications for the future. If all CFC production were to stop today, it could take at least 40 to 100 years for the ozone-depleting chemicals to leave the air.

International Attention. Nations and industries are working together to protect the ozone layer. International treaties such as the 1987 Montreal Protocol call for an eventual halt in the production of ozone-depleting chemicals (CFCs). Even if production is halted in the target years in the early 21st century, it is not known how long it will take for the hole in the ozone layer to repair itself, nor is it known by what means this can be accomplished.

RADIATION AND HUMANS

The Sun emits energy, which is dispersed throughout the Solar System in many forms. There are visible rays, such as those seen during a rainbow; invisible rays, such as ultraviolet light; and other forms of energy, such as infrared (heat) rays. Radio waves, gamma rays, cosmic rays, and other solar emissions also affect the Earth's surface.

Radioactivity was discovered by the French scientist Antoine Henri Becquerel (1852-1908) in 1896. He accidentally placed a sample of uranium (U) on a photographic plate that was wrapped in black paper. When he looked at the plate later, it had darkened, as if it had been exposed to light. Becquerel guessed that the uranium was sending out an invisible emission similar to visible light waves. Becquerel termed the emission *radioactivity*. Later, three major types of radiation were identified—alpha (α), beta (ß), and gamma (γ). Though all can be called radiation, they are actually quite different from one another: alpha radiation is a stream of particles (helium nuclei); beta radiation is again a stream of particles, but much smaller ones (high-energy electrons or positrons); and gamma radiation is a high-energy form of electromagnetic radiation.

Electromagnetic radiation was eventually defined by Albert Einstein (1879-1955) as the transmission of packages of energy called photons. Although photons are often called particles of light, they are thought not to be actual particles with mass. Max Planck (1858-1947), a German physicist, described the energy of a single photon as proportional to the frequency of radiation. Therefore, the higher the frequency of a particular wavelength, the

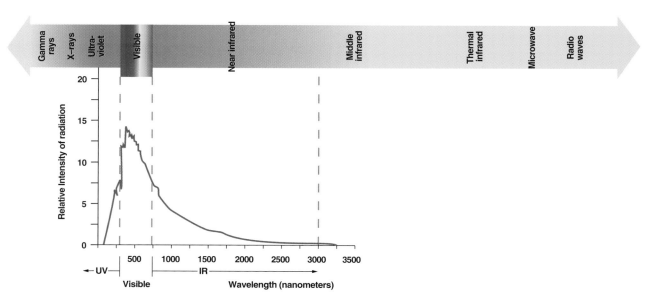

The electromagnetic spectrum from the Sun stretches far beyond the small portion we can see, but the peak amount of energy falls in the visible range.

greater the energy of a single photon in that wavelength. One photon of UV light is 10 million times stronger than one photon of a radio wave. Gamma radiation is stronger yet and can move through almost any substance, occasionally damaging delicate materials such as human cells.

Radiation and radioactivity occur in nature. Radon (Rn), a colorless, odorless gas, is a naturally occurring substance that happens to be highly radioactive. There are also many human-caused sources of radioactivity. A nuclear power plant uses nuclear elements to create power, and under normal conditions little radiation escapes. Although difficult to believe, a trip in an airplane exposes humans to more than 10 times the amount of radiation incurred over an entire lifetime from nuclear-power-plant emissions. An accident that did release some radiation in 1979 at the Three Mile Island nuclear power plant in Middletown, Pennsylvania, exposed workers and residents to less radiation than a single X-ray.

Harmful Effects. When radiation is received in large doses, however, the results can be devastating. In 1986, people living near the Chernobyl power plant in Russia were poisoned and killed from radiation sickness when a nuclear meltdown occurred. Survivors gave birth to children with severe birth defects. Radiation carries a huge amount of energy which, upon contact with the cells of a living organism, disrupts the building blocks of cellular structures. Radiation in heavy doses can irreversibly alter and mutate chromosomes and genes, giving rise to birth defects.

The amount of harm to cells depends on the level of exposure to radiation. The energy absorbed by cells is called a radiation absorbed dose, or a rad. A rad is multiplied by the strength of a particular form of radiation, which produces a roentgen equivalent man, or rem. A rem is the dosage of radiation that causes the same biological effect as 1 roentgen of X-ray or gamma-ray dosage. Smaller quantities are measured in millirems. During a normal human lifetime,

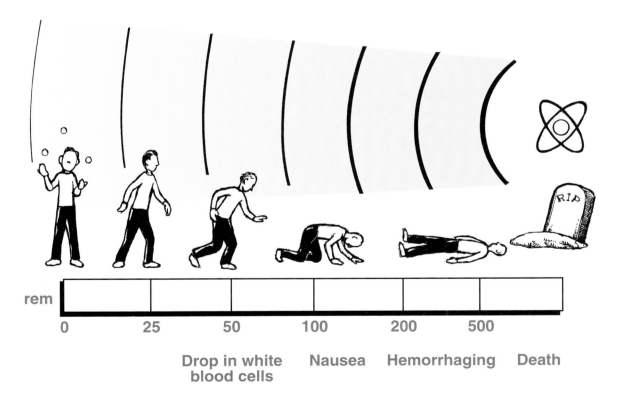

rem					
0	25	50	100	200	500

Drop in white blood cells   Nausea   Hemorrhaging   Death

The human body responds to increasing doses of radiation by mild symptoms at first, then serious internal bleeding (hemorrhaging), and finally death.

an individual is exposed to about 500 millirems of ionizing radiation per year. Radiation exposure differs based on location, altitude, or proximity to a source of radiation. For example, a person traveling in a plane receives about 0.5 millirem per trip, whereas an individual spending life isolated in a house at sea level would receive a total of only about 25 millirems over the course of an entire year.

One form of radiation comes from ultraviolet light. In industry, UV light is used to preserve some types of food, such as tomatoes. UV light is responsible for the human production of vitamin D and a skin pigment called melanin, which gives humans the ability to tan. When any organism is exposed to the Sun, some amount of UV light is falling on and penetrating it. Depending on the intensity of the UV light, as well as the sensitivity of the organism, UV light can render different amounts of damage. Humans with light skin, for example, produce less melanin and are more prone to skin cancers than humans with darker skin. Those with more melanin are better protected from the effects of solar radiation. No matter how dark a person's skin may be, however, all humans are advised to apply lotions that block the absorption of UV light from the Sun. Many studies have concluded that with a reduction in the ozone layer, an increased incidence of nonmelanoma skin cancer will occur. People of similar melanin quantities living in sunny zones report about twice as many incidents of nonmelanoma skin cancer each year than people residing in colder areas with weaker doses of sunshine.

Plants react to UV radiation by cutting down on growth. Phytoplankton, tiny ocean-dwelling plants

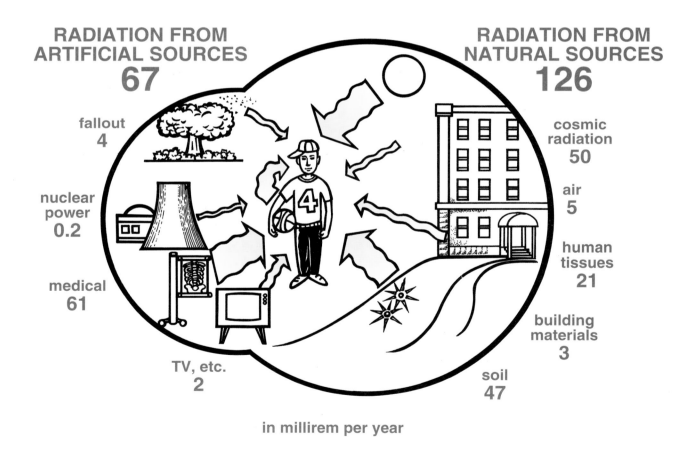

RADIATION FROM ARTIFICIAL SOURCES 67

fallout 4

nuclear power 0.2

medical 61

TV, etc. 2

RADIATION FROM NATURAL SOURCES 126

cosmic radiation 50

air 5

human tissues 21

building materials 3

soil 47

in millirem per year

We receive radiation from many sources. About a third are human-created sources, and the remaining two-thirds are natural sources.

Deliberate tanning at the beach seems to be a 20th-century habit, as here on Australia's Gold Coast. Yet it is only in the 20th century that we have learned of the Sun's role in skin cancer.

that are a vital food source for thousands of animals, are susceptible to disease caused by UV radiation. If UV radiation were to affect these organisms on a large scale, the world's food chain could be disrupted. The phytoplankton in the oceans are also important links in the global carbon cycle. They absorb carbon dioxide, removing it from the atmosphere where it could contribute to global warming. The depletion of phytoplankton could, therefore, alter the delicate balance of the atmosphere.

Although sunlight is important to all creatures and plants on Earth, predictions and theories concerning increased heat and light energy in the biosphere show the potential for environmental damage. Through further research on the causes and effects of the greenhouse effect, global warming, and the depletion of the ozone layer, humans can attempt to reverse any negative impacts they have made upon the atmosphere.

Sources

Browne, Malcolm W. "Most precise gauge yet points to global warming," *New York Times* (December 20, 1994).

Christopherson, Robert W. *Geosystems.* New York: Macmillan Publishing Co., 1992.

Doyle, Kathleen. "Ozone Alert," *E: The Environmental Magazine* (July/August 1994).

"Global Warming: Beyond Termites," *Science News* 145 (June 25, 1994).

Monastersky, Richard. "Life Blooms on Floor of Deep Siberian Lake," *Science News* 138 (August 18, 1990).

Schwartz, A. Truman, et al. *Chemistry in Context.* Dubuque, IA: Wm. C. Brown Publishers, 1994. ©American Chemical Society.

Stevens, William K. "Emissions Must Be Cut to Avert Shift in Climate, Panel Says," *New York Times* (September 20, 1994).

CHAPTER THREE

Properties of Energy

Throughout human history, energy has been quantified, explained, categorized, and generated. While searching for explanations for the motion of objects and celestial bodies, early scientists and engineers discovered the laws of gravity, motion, heat, and mechanical action. Several theories were tested and proven by scientists such as Copernicus, Newton, and Einstein. Although their "laws" may later have been questioned or even disproved, they defined many of the issues and gave modern science a strong foundation upon which to describe the motion and energy of the universe.

EARLY STUDIES OF ENERGY AND MOTION

Aristotle. One of the first scientists to study energy and motion, or at least one of the first whose writings survive, was Aristotle (384–322 B.C.). This ancient Greek philosopher contributed to almost every field of science, from mathematics and logic to physics and biology. Whereas his own teacher, Plato, favored abstract thinking, Aristotle taught observation and gathered museum collections.

Aristotle's writings became the first studies of what we call gravity. He suggested that things moved in certain directions because each has its own "proper place" and moves toward it until stopped. Drop a ball, and it falls down until it comes to rest on the ground. Once rest is achieved, all motion stops. Solid, "earthy" objects and liquid, "watery" ones all move downward toward the center of the Earth. Air rises to its proper place in the atmosphere. Fire, too, rises, until greeted by air currents that make fire dance unpredictably.

But if these motions were natural, what if something, say a ball, is thrown in a direction not "natural" to it? A new theory would be required to explain the movement—the idea of a force to set it in motion and give it little pushes along the way to keep it moving. Aristotle called this forced movement "violent motion" and applied it to all objects that lacked a "soul," that is, that could not move on their own power.

Aristotle's views were widely accepted, but ultimately may have retarded rather than advanced our development of more exact ideas. The "proper-place" concept perhaps delayed Newton's universal gravity. The "violent-motion" concept made it hard to imagine anything moving without being pushed by something along the way. This made it hard to describe the movements of planets with no obvious agents to propel them in empty space. But if Aristotle was a philosophical scientist whose ideas sometimes failed later testing, he defined for centuries the European way of thinking about motion and energy.

Galileo Galilei. Centuries later, Italian mathematical physicist Galileo Galilei (1564-1642) studied Aristotle's philosophy and, finding it inadequate to describe physical motion, began to explore the physical reasons behind motion and rest. Aristotle's ideas about violent force as the prime mover of an object explained how an object moves in the first place but did not explain why an object would continue to move, seemingly of its own volition. How, for instance, could a planet stay in motion out in space with nothing around to keep pushing it? Galileo saw how the problem of motion was linked to our knowledge of the heavens and pursued both halves of the inquiry. Today, he is known mainly for two things: the discoveries he made by turning a telescope on the heavens and his championship of a scientific method that combined actual experiments with mathematical description. He did not invent the telescope, but when he heard of it, he made one of his own, then many more, which were distributed widely. In 1610, around the planet Jupiter, he saw four tiny lights that changed position night after night: they were moons of Jupiter. You can see them too—with binoculars. (Today's birdwatching binoculars are commonly 7 to 10 power; that is, they make things look that many times as long. You can easily beat Galileo's first telescope of only 3 power. His last, of 32 power, would be a challenge.)

This discovery proved to be more than just another new fact. The tiny moons wheeling around great Jupiter recalled that old Greek picture that Copernicus had envisioned: small planets orbiting a massive Sun. If Galileo and anyone who cared to look through a telescope could see a miniature Copernican Solar System around Jupiter, then perhaps an entire Sun-centered Solar System might seem more workable. Even as he championed the Sun-centered system, Galileo experimented in more

Earthbound ways. He early timed the swaying of a hanging church chandelier, and years later used what he found to write a mathematical description of swinging objects, or pendulums (helping make pendulum clocks possible). He rolled balls down slopes, or inclined planes, and dropped them off heights to observe motion in the real world, finding mathematical ways to describe these motions. The often-told story that he dropped balls off the leaning tower of Pisa may be true, though there is no evidence that he assembled any great audience of dignitaries to watch him do it, as the story usually insists. In any case, it would be hard to get a precise law out of real measurements of rolling or falling balls in a real world: you would have to account for things like friction, air resistance, and imperfections in making the balls. Galileo saw past the actual, imperfect results to a more abstract, mathematical description that was continued after his lifetime in the work of Newton, Einstein, and many others.

Today, the physical laws that we use to understand our planet and its ecosystems, the movement of water and air, the erosion of soil, still owe a debt to the early experimenters before and after Galileo. We remember Galileo himself both for his own discoveries and for his demonstration of the usefulness of matching observation with mathematical tools. But Galileo in his lifetime was a controversial figure who led a troubled life. Sometimes he was supported by powerful people, even a pope. Sometimes he offended them. In the end, he was forced to live in partial isolation, with a few assistants, but forbidden to teach publicly, especially on the Copernican question.

Sir Isaac Newton. Not until the work of British physicist and mathematician Sir Isaac Newton (1642-1727) did scientists begin to understand the complex laws of the universe and describe them in a mathematical way that enabled them to make valid predictions. At the age of 22, Newton moved out of London during the plague epidemic and set up a laboratory on his farm to conduct experiments on light. Over the next several years, Newton devised his laws of motion and theory of gravity, which he discussed in a book called the *Philosophiae*

Working in the 17th century, Sir Isaac Newton may have thought of himself as a philosopher rather than scientist, yet his insights into light and gravity opened new paths in physics.

Naturalis Principia Mathematica (*Mathematical Principles of Natural Philosophy*), otherwise known as Newton's *Principia*. The book was published in 1687, marking the first time people began to understand motion and gravity, both on Earth and in the skies, seeing them as different aspects of one set of "laws," or mathematical descriptions.

Newton's First Law. Newton's ideas were based on the work of Galileo. Newton's first law states that an object at rest remains at rest unless some force acts on it. The law also states that an object moving at a constant speed and in a straight line will continue to do so until a force acts on it, stopping, slowing, or altering its motion. In other words, a moving body is at "rest" as long as its motion is constant and in a single direction. A cannonball shot from a cannon, for example, will move through the air in a straight line unless air provides

resistance to slow it down or unless gravity pulls the cannonball to the ground, where all motion is halted. Similarly, a spinning top will stop moving when resistance from air and friction between the ground and the top cause it to slow down and fall to the ground. Newton further concluded that planets moving through the universe encounter no friction and will continue to move straight ahead or on a curved path unless met with some type of resistance, such as an impact with an asteroid.

Newton's Second Law. Newton's second law, the law of acceleration, states that a change in motion is proportional to the force that sets an object into the changed motion. In other words, if a force is applied to an object, the object will accelerate in the direction of the force. The greater the force, the greater the acceleration. The heavier the object, however, the harder it is to increase the rate of acceleration. A pencil, for example, is easier to push than a book. Furthermore, an object will move in a straight line from the point at which it is hit until another force acts upon it. This means that an object can be moved by different degrees of strength, and multiple movers can force the object to move at different speeds and directions. Newton claimed that a destination could be predicted for a moving object if the measure of the force moving the object and the direction in which it was pushed were known.

Newton's Third Law. Newton's third law states that for every action there is an equal and opposite reaction. In other words, if one object exerts a force on another object, the other object exerts an equal force in the opposite direction on the first object. This law explains the motion of jet airplanes—the exhaust from the engines pushes on the air, forcing the jet in the opposite direction. It also explains how objects remain on a table rather than falling to the ground. For example, gravity exerts a downward force on a book resting on a table. The table exerts an equal and opposite force on the book, keeping it from falling to the ground.

Newton was one of the greatest scientists of all time. Aside from his work on the *Principia*, he also studied light and mathematics. He was the first to dis-

The swing of the wrecking ball carries energy that is transferred to the brick wall at the moment the ball hits it. If this force is stronger than the forces holding the bricks together, the wall collapses.

cover the colors of the spectrum as seen through a prism. He theorized correctly that light can be described as a stream of tiny particles, or corpuscles, that travel in straight lines at great speeds. This theory came to be known as the corpuscle theory. In 1669, Newton created calculus, a branch of mathematics that helped scientists work out very complex problems having values that keep changing, such as the problem of describing the movement of a planet in a curved path around the Sun. Thus, calculus became the first good mathematical tool to describe the workings of gravity. In the same year, he invented the reflecting telescope. By the end of his life, Newton had provided the world with a foundation of concepts and a set of mathematical tools with which to study the universe.

FORMS OF ENERGY

Energy is broken down into kinetic and potential forms. Consider a book resting on a table's edge as an example: potential energy is the measure of the book's ability to fall off the table and be in motion. It can be thought of as the energy required to lift the book up onto the table in the first place—energy that can be gotten back and used by letting the book drop off to the floor, releasing its energy as the impact, force, and bang when the book hits. Kinetic energy is what we call this actual energy that can be experienced or harnessed from the book while it is in motion. A reservoir behind a dam is another example of potential energy. When the water is released from the reservoir, kinetic energy can be taken from the powerful flow of the downhill rush of water.

Storage and Release of Energy. Earth and its inhabitants use several forms of energy every day. In the environment, chemical energy drives life cycles as well as energy cycles. During a chemical reaction, energy may be either absorbed or released. An example of a process producing chemical energy in the environment is photosynthesis. During this reaction, plants absorb and store solar energy in their cells. The stored energy is then released to other organisms which eat or use the plants as fuel. Fossil fuels, such as coal and oil, are the remains of ancient plants (or sometimes animals); the energy the plants stored

while living can still be retrieved from the fossil fuel millions of years later through combustion. A rare version of combustion is known as spontaneous combustion, which refers to the unpredictable explosion of some animal and vegetable oils. Oil-soaked rags and paper have been known to catch on fire spontaneously, as have coal and charcoal stored in large piles.

Conversion of Energy. The most important quality of energy is that it can be converted from one form to another. At least three types of energy are used together in the simple act of opening and closing a door. First, chemical energy stored in the body is used to activate hand muscles to force a knob to turn and the door to open. Second, the force applied to open the door requires mechanical energy. Third, if the person then slams the door shut, sound energy is created. If the hinges are rusty, the person may even turn some energy into the squeak of the hinge.

Electricity. Another form of energy is electrical energy. Electric currents are forms of energy that drive machinery and power modern appliances. Humans experience one form of electrical energy on cold, dry days when a comb pulled through hair makes the strands stand on end or when touching a metal car door produces an electric "shock." Electricity is produced when other forms of energy, such as heat or solar energy, are harnessed and transformed into electrical energy. Electric power plants create electricity by driving huge turbines that turn an electric generator, changing the mechanical energy in the turbine to electrical energy. Solar energy can create electrical energy through a photovoltaic cell, which uses photons in sunlight to displace enough electrons on a cell to create a stream of electrons, or an electrical current. Electrical energy can also be produced from nuclear energy. By splitting an atom, energy is released and converted to heat energy, which is then used to produce steam that drives turbines to produce electricity.

Electrical energy is the flow of a series of charged particles in a circuit. The measure of the energy available to move charges in a circuit is called voltage. Electric current is produced when positive and negative ions are combined to form a chain of ions. Negative ions are attracted to positive charges, and positive ions are attracted to negative charges. This attraction creates a flow of energy known as an electric current. An example of electric current is the energy that flows through a battery. The negative electrons are attracted to the positive terminal of a battery, and a flow of electrons generates an electric current.

Measuring Energy. To measure all the various kinds of energy on the same scale, we need a unit that can fit them all. One approach is to imagine all the kinds of energy turned to heat, then measure the heat. The Btu, or British thermal unit, is the standard measurement of heat energy, whether produced by electricity, by burning coal, or by any other means. One Btu is the amount of heat energy required to raise the temperature of 1 pound of water 1° Fahrenheit. Large amounts of heat energy are measured in quads, an abbreviation for 1 quadrillion Btu. One quad is equivalent to about 172 million barrels of oil.

The metric method for measuring heat is by calories or kilocalories. One kilocalorie is the amount of energy needed to raise the temperature of 1 kilogram of water 1° Centigrade. When people speak of eating so many "calories" a day, they are actually referring to what the scientist would call kilocalories. The true scientific "calorie" is too small for convenience—we would be measuring out our daily diet in millions of calories. In scientific terms, then, our food "calories," are really kilocalories, but the principle is the same: we are measuring *heat*—the heat that the food could be turned into when our bodies "burn" it for energy.

Watts are units to measure work. A 40-watt bulb uses 40 watts of electrical power to provide illumination. Electric companies bill customers for their use of electricity based on watt-hours. Most often, electricity measurements are calculated in larger units called kilowatts and kilowatt-hours. One kilowatt-hour is the use of 1 kilowatt over a one-hour period. In the United States, an average home uses about 8,900 kilowatt-hours of electricity every year. Multiplying that figure by the number of electricity consumers in the 50 states, the nation uses more than 2.8 billion kilowatt-hours of electricity annual-

ly. Instruments called single-phase watt-hour meters are located on the outside of most homes and display the amount of kilowatt-hours of electricity consumed. The device is actually a small electric motor that runs at a speed proportional to the amount of current passing through it. Inside are coils and a disk that drives a series of dials indicating the kilowatt-hour measurements. These dials are periodically checked by the utility company in order to charge accurate fees for electricity usage.

Magnetism and Electricity. Magnetic fields can also produce electric currents. In 1820, Dutch scientist Hans Christian Oersted (1777–1851) discovered that if the magnetized needle of a compass is near a current-carrying wire, the needle will realign itself. All forms of magnetism come from a moving electrical charge. A videocassette recorder (VCR) is an example of the use of a magnetic field creating an electric current. To record a program, varying electrical currents in a tape head (an electromagnet) realign the magnetized particles on the cassette tape to match the magnetic field produced by the current. To play the program back, the VCR uses the magnetic pattern that had been laid down on the tape to generate new electrical impulses to run the TV, bringing the original program back on the screen.

Heat. Most often, electrical and other forms of energy are produced by burning fuel to produce heat energy. Once thought of as a kind of fluid, heat was studied by scientists such as Newton and Galileo. In actuality, heat energy is the kinetic energy of the individual molecules of an object. The faster the molecules of an object move, the more heat there is. Heat can be used to do work. For example, utilities burn coal to heat water, which in turn creates steam that drives turbines to make electricity.

THE LAWS OF THERMODYNAMICS

The word *thermodynamics* means "the movement of heat." The laws of thermodynamics are used to study how heat travels from one place to another and how heat is converted to other forms of energy. Three basic laws were put forth by scientists in the 1800s. A fourth law, the "zeroth law," has recently been added.

A meter records the amount of electricity consumed by a household, whether they live in a city apartment or a rural log cabin.

Factories convert energy from fuel to heat and work. In the process they emit many plumes of gases into the air. Just by looking, it can be impossible to tell what is a harmless cloud of water vapor and what is harmful pollution in the making.

The First Law of Thermodynamics. The first law of thermodynamics states that energy is neither created nor destroyed—the energy of the universe is constant. This is sometimes called the law of conservation of energy. The first law also defines the term *heat energy*, and describes how energy can be converted into other forms. The first law can be applied to fuels. Almost all fuels used today, such as coal, oil, gasoline, and alcohol, give up their energy through combustion. Heat energy is generated to do work. Work is done when energy is transferred from a system to its surroundings through mechanical means, such as when gasoline is combusted in an engine and energy is supplied to the car's piston shaft. When this occurs, heat flows from a system to its surroundings. A modern power plant is a good example of how combustible fuels release energy to create work. Potential energy that has been stored in the chemical bonds of fossil fuels for millions of years is first converted to heat energy. When burned, the fuels release heat that is absorbed by water, which turns into steam. This heat is then converted to mechanical energy in the turbine that turns the generator, changing the

ENVIROBIT

Every year, the United States consumes about 80 quads of energy.

mechanical energy into electrical energy. Although no matter is lost or gained during these transformations, there is still enough energy changed in form that modern machines cannot adequately use and handle all the heat and energy that is created.

Increased energy efficiency is the goal of engineers and scientists alike. Most machines waste much of the energy fed to them. Energy efficiency is defined as the ratio of output energy delivered to a system, such as a machine, to the amount of input energy supplied, such as gasoline. No machine can completely convert heat to work. Power plants experience an average heat loss of about 60%. Some energy is always lost to the design of a plant or machine, which loses heat

energy to friction and heat leakage. In an automobile engine, for example, much of the fuel that is burned in the combustion engine is released as waste heat, which does nothing to power the car's pistons. This is the same reaction that occurs at a power plant—waste heat is emitted to the atmosphere as steam or is released into ponds or streams as warm water.

If power plants are necessarily going to produce heat as well as the electricity we want, one thing we can do to be more efficient is to find a way to use that heat, to generate—or cogenerate—useful heat right alongside useful electricity. Thus, one way to boost energy efficiency in a power plant is to install a cogeneration system in an existing power plant. In one arrangement, the cogeneration system catches the waste heat from power plants and uses it to heat another water source to make steam that drives electricity-producing turbines.

Energy efficiency is measurable in nature as well. Photosynthetic reactions are only about 1% efficient; that is, about 1% of the solar energy that hits the leaves of a plant is converted to chemical energy.

Efficiency can be maximized by changes in the machine or in the fuel used. Consider an automobile as an example: aerodynamic design is taken into account when engineering the car's body. Because more than 60% of the fuel and power used to drive at 89 kilometers per hour (55 miles per hour) is lost to wind resistance, changes in the body to reduce drag, or air friction, have helped improve the car's efficiency in terms of gas mileage. Engineers continually search for ways to decrease the weight of an automobile, since lower weight means less matter to propel forward, thus increasing fuel efficiency.

The Second Law of Thermodynamics. According to the first law of thermodynamics, energy can be transformed, but it does not describe *how* one type of energy can be transformed into other types of energy, say heat into work. The second law of thermodynamics does. While there are many ways to interpret the second law, the main idea is that it is impossible to completely convert heat into work. If the first law says, "You can't get something for nothing," the second law says, "You can't even break even." In every transfer from heat to work, you lose some waste heat and get no work from it.

Machines are created to do work for humans but they will always waste energy. Some machines are only 5% efficient. Even the best are seldom over 30% efficient. *Most* of the heat energy goes to waste. This second-law truth makes it environmentally important that machines be designed to maximize energy efficiency and keep friction losses low so that they can do a lot of work while consuming the least amount of energy.

If heat is such a problem, would it be possible to make an engine that works *without* starting from heat? Fuel cells could make it possible to do this. They convert a fuel's chemical energy directly to electricity without combustion or moving parts. With fuel cells we should be able to avoid much less loss from waste heat than with today's combustion engines.

The movement of heat from a warmer to a colder body is experienced every day and is the essence of thermodynamics. When we touch a cool surface, such as a cold glass of water, heat from our hands flows out of our palms and fingers and is absorbed into the glass, warming it and the water. This flow of heat explains why placing a pot of liquid or food on a stove produces boiling liquids and hot foods, though it is only the pot that touches the stove.

Waste heat serves no useful purpose and can be harmful to the environment. For example, urban heat islands are areas that have a warmer-than-average climate because of emissions of heat from such sources as people, industries, homes, and automobiles. In bodies of water, industrial emissions of hot water can spur algal blooms, or a breakout of algae growth, which can deplete water of its supply of oxygen. As a result, aquatic life can suffocate. Sometimes, however, excess heat in a body of water can warm an area enough so that it can support life where once it was too cold. At least it can support it until one day the plant shuts down for repairs and many of the creatures die of sudden cold.

The first and second laws of thermodynamics give insight into the use and transformation of energy and how these relate to environmental issues. For example, humans rely heavily on fossil fuels that

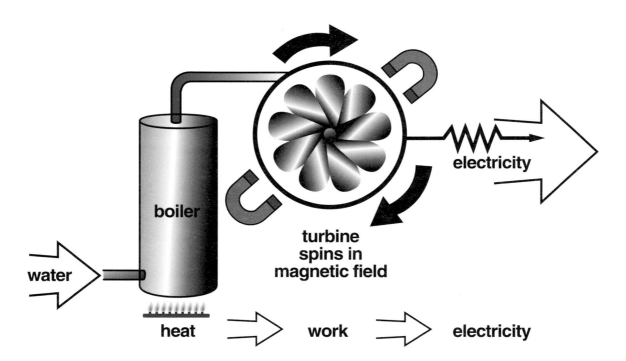

Power plants transform heat energy to work energy (turning a turbine) and then to electrical energy.

This cryogenic, or freezing, chamber was designed to preserve individuals at the brink of death who chose to be frozen so as to have a chance of being thawed out years later when—and if—a cure for their disease would be available.

were created over the course of millions of years and are available in finite quantities. Because fossil fuels burn well to create heat energy, which can then do work, we see them as excellent fuels. But looking at fossil fuels through the eyes of a thermodynamicist exposes another picture: the fuels provide a one-way energy flow with lots of waste heat. Once fossil-fuel supplies are gone, it is impossible to re-create them. If we want them some day as sources of chemicals, we may regret burning them now, or at least burning so much of them in inefficient, heat-wasting machines.

Other applications of thermodynamics exist in specialized sciences. One example within the field of chemistry is called chemical thermodynamics, the study of the energy changes that occur during chemical reactions. In chemistry, thermodynamics is used to predict chemical reactions, which is helpful when the reaction is highly theoretical or too difficult or dangerous to carry out in a laboratory setting. On occasion this ability to predict reactions can help settle environmental issues, such as how hazardous or nuclear wastes will react together during long-term storage.

The Third Law of Thermodynamics and Cryogenics. Cryogenics is the study of temperatures colder than those naturally found on Earth. At these unnaturally cold temperatures, matter undergoes unexpected phase shifts. Air, for example, can become a liquid, and organic tissues could freeze instantly. Matter responds strangely when in a cryogenic state—electric currents may flow continuously and liquids run uphill against the force of gravity.

Since the temperature of a gas, liquid, or solid is the measure of how quickly its atoms are moving, atoms and molecules in a warm mass of air (or anything else) move faster than in a cold mass of air. When matter is cooled, its atoms slow down. If a substance were cooled to a low enough temperature, they would show no motion at all. This temperature, known as absolute zero, occurs at -273.16°C (-459.69°F) and is the same for all forms of matter. The term *absolute zero* implies that no

colder temperature could exist; however, this is true only in a carefully defined sense, governed by

what is called the third law of thermodynamics. This states that the "disorder" of a perfect crystal—mainly the movement of its atoms—decreases as absolute zero is approached. At absolute zero—which we can never reach—all heat would be gone. The motion of atoms that we call heat would stop (though atoms might still have internal energy within their atomic particles).

Although scientists have been unable to reach all the way to absolute zero, they have come very close and on the way have made discoveries of great potential for resolving environmental issues. Chief of these discoveries from cold-temperature research is superconductivity—the ability of some very cold metals, ceramics, and other substances to conduct electricity without the usual losses. If all the world's power lines could be built of such materials and chilled down to operate this way (without costing too much), energy savings would be immense. Environmental damage from power transmission would drop sharply.

Matter that has been cryogenically frozen is so cold that the Celsius and Fahrenheit temperature scales require large negative numbers, which are not convenient for measuring the low temperatures. Scientists therefore replace those more familiar scales by the Kelvin and Rankine temperature scales. These scales use absolute zero temperature as their zero point in the same way the Celsius scale uses the freezing point of water under standard conditions as its zero point. The Kelvin scale uses a range of degrees the same size

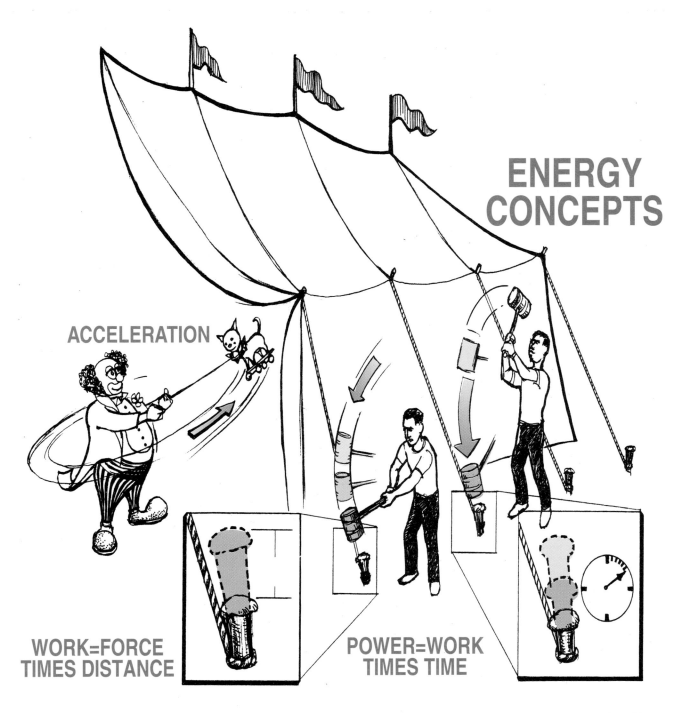

ENERGY CONCEPTS

ACCELERATION

WORK=FORCE
TIMES DISTANCE

POWER=WORK
TIMES TIME

SYSTEM OF UNITS		WORK	=	FORCE times DISTANCE		
International System (SI)	cgs (small)	erg	=	dyne	•	centimeter
	mks (large)	joule	=	newton	•	meter
U.S. Common Measure		foot-pound	=	pound	•	foot

Understanding environmental questions often requires understanding the physics (or chemistry) behind them.

ENVIROBIT

If fuel cells could be mass-produced economically, it has been suggested that they could make internal-combustion engines obsolete early in the 21st century. Cars that use fuel cells could be up to three times as efficient as those powered by conventional combustion engines and would emit virtually no pollutants.

as those on the Celsius scale; the Rankine method uses a range of degrees the same size as those on the Fahrenheit scale—they just move their zero points down.

Cryogenics is used for many industrial purposes. The liquefaction of gases is used in the scientific and industrial realms for the distillation of pure gases, such as oxygen (O), nitrogen (N), and neon (Ne). Transporting liquids is much easier and safer than moving gas, since gas must be contained under tremendous pressure. U.S. space shuttles use liquid hydrogen–oxygen fuels to propel them into space. Such fuels are relatively safe to handle and weigh considerably less than other types of fuel. In hospitals, cryogenically prepared liquid nitrogen is used to surgically remove cancer cells in a process called cryosurgery. Cryotherapy is another medical technique that involves freezing blood vessels that are damaging the retina of a patient's eye.

The future of cryogenics rests in many applications in such disciplines as health and medicine, engineering, physics, and space programs. Surely applications can be found in environmental science, but it may be the next generation of scientists who find them. While researchers are more familiar with the physics behind higher levels of heat and energy, cryogenics is a relatively new science that has much potential for the future.

The Fourth Law of Thermodynamics. The fourth law of thermodynamics, sometimes called the zeroth law, describes a state called thermal equilibrium. The law is based on the fact that if two objects at different temperatures are brought together, the

heat from the hot object will flow into the cooler one. The objects will continue to absorb and emit energy at different rates until their temperatures are the same. When the two objects reach equal temperatures, they will emit and absorb energy at the same rate and be in thermal equilibrium. The zeroth law further states that if two objects are in thermal equilibrium with a third object, then the two are in thermal equilibrium with each other.

Because of the laws of thermodynamics, scientists understand how heat and cold affect objects and systems. We know that heat energy is responsible for the movement and work capacity of machines, and we know that disorder is a natural state in the universe. Moreover, the laws of thermodynamics provide engineers, designers, physicists, and chemists with the rules that govern the functioning of machines and engines.

THE CONCEPT OF RELATIVITY

The concept of relativity was presented by German-American physicist Albert Einstein (1879-1955) in the special theory of relativity in 1905 and refined under the general theory of relativity in 1916. The 1905 version is called "special" because it was developed for the special case of simple, straight-line movement, without changes of direction or speed. The general theory of 1916 can be applied to the more general case of any kind of motion, even curved or accelerated motion. That means it can explain the complicated movements of planets and galaxies.

Einstein's writings changed forever our way of looking at the universe. They introduced the concept of space-time. They showed that matter itself could be converted into energy, making possible what has since been called nuclear power.

Einstein's theory of 1905 came at a time when changes in scientific theory had to be made. Experiments in the late 19th century had found problems with the old Galilean physics—problems with the speeds of things, especially light. It sometimes seemed that light particles did not obey the same rules as other moving objects, which confused and dismayed scientists.

Einstein's theory of relativity showed that some of Newton's laws were not universally true but were just the beginning of broader mathematical descriptions that could apply to the great speeds and masses of the heavens as well as to ordinary life on Earth.

The problem was a matter of perception. Suppose you are standing in a field and you throw a ball in front of you. It moves away from you with a certain speed. Now you start running and again throw the ball. You throw it from you just as fast as before, but now the ball has a faster speed across the field: your running speed plus the ball's thrown speed. This adding of speeds had not been questioned since Galileo and Newton. It works well enough with ordinary objects like balls and with ordinary speeds like the fastest you can throw. But let us speed up the example. Suppose that the thrower is now the Earth sweeping along its orbit instead of you running in a field and that Earth sends out a beam of light ahead of it. You on Earth see the beam of light move away at (of course) the speed of light. But someone out in space ought, by the addition rule, to see the light moving even faster across the "field" of space: the light's speed plus Earth's. Thus by sticking to the speed-adding rules we used for balls, we would seem to make light move faster than the speed of light. But it never does.

In 1887 a famous experiment measured the speed of light very accurately. The experiment found the speed of light to be the same no matter which direction the light was moving. This surprised scientists. They expected that light would behave like a ball thrown in a field, moving faster or slower depending on whether the thrower was running or not when the ball was thrown. Was something wrong with the math? Was there in fact something wrong with all the laws of physics that had seemed so settled?

At this point Einstein stepped in. He accepted that the experiment was correct. Light traveling through the vacuum of space did travel at only one set speed, just as the experiment said. It did not matter that two observers might be in different places and moving relative to each other (someone on Earth and someone in space). Both observers would somehow have to measure the same light speed.

So what was it that just offset any effect of the two observers' relative motions? Einstein found that he could get the math to match the experiment only if he assumed something drastic: that the very rulers, scales, and clocks people used to measure with can subtly change. He found that everything worked out if a meter steadily got a certain amount shorter as an object sped up; similarly, the kilogram became heavier and the second longer (as seen by someone watching you from outside, not by you yourself). The effects of measurement and motion would just balance, and you would have no trouble describing light by the same physics you use to describe objects.

These explanations changed the realm of physics forever. People were not sure it made any sense at all. But new experiments backed up Einstein's explanations and predictions. An odd movement of Mercury in orbit or the bending of a star's light as it passed near the Sun was found to match Einstein's predictions. Even tiny subatomic particles, if accelerated to nearly the speed of light, were found to become more massive. This leads to the fact that no material object can move quite as fast as the speed of light in a vacuum. If any material object approached such a speed, it would become too massive for all the energy in the universe to accelerate it all the way. Light particles, or photons, can go that fast only because they are not in this sense "material" objects. Photons do not exist sitting still. They are thought to have no mass to begin with, so their mass cannot increase when they speed up. Thus, there is no reason why they cannot reach the speed of light.

Einstein called this new kind of warped space that made all these things understandable space-time. Imagine how a stretched rubber sheet would sag down if you set a bowling ball on it. Call the ball a planet, star, or galaxy, and you can treat its gravity as the warped space-time around it. Things move in curved paths, not the straight lines of Greek geometry. Heavy objects, or very fast objects, have much warpage about them; mass and energy are in some sense the same in space-time. Furthermore, energy and mass each can change into the other according

CASE STUDY: PERPETUAL MOTION

Since the time humans first realized that enormous amounts of fuel are needed to maintain mechanical processes, attempts have been made to design machines that put out more energy than they take in. If it were possible to create a machine that generated more work-producing energy than was supplied to it in other forms of energy, it would be called a perpetual-motion machine.

Because of the laws of thermodynamics, which state that energy is neither created nor destroyed, that some amount of energy is always lost when one form of energy is converted to another, and that heat flows from a warm body into a colder one, it is impossible for the total energy output of a machine to exceed its total input of energy. A perpetual-motion machine attempts to use only one dose of energy, rather than a continual input, to carry out work. This is impossible, however, due to friction and heat, or energy, loss. Friction, whether with some solid object, the air, or a liquid, converts some mechanical energy to heat energy. This heat energy cannot be totally recovered and recycled to power the machine. All machines are eventually stopped by frictional forces.

Before the first and second laws of thermodynamics were understood, inventors, scientists, and engineers sought to create a machine that could use an input of energy over and over again without any degradation. Popular technologies at the time were endlessly turning wheels powered by gravity and waterwheels that rotated under water by the upward force of the liquid. But because friction and heat loss are always involved with the motion of an object, perpetual-motion machines are an impossibility.

Since the laws of thermodynamics were presented in the late 1800s, perpetual-motion machines have met with much skepticism. Since 1918, the U.S. government's patent office has denied any patent requests for perpetual-motion machines.

Requests are still submitted, but no patents have been issued. Today, these machines are used in scam operations. Many inventors solicit money for an invention they know will not function, thus stealing money from investors who do not understand the laws of thermodynamics.

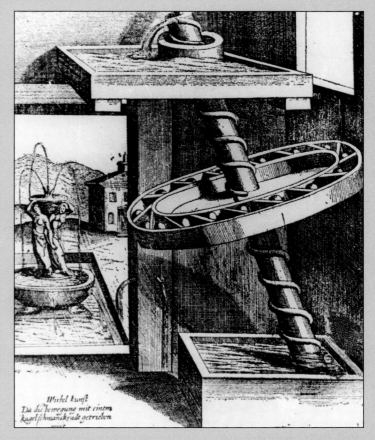

Perpetual-motion machines do not exist and cannot exist, yet people are continually inventing them—or claiming to. When looked at closely, they always reveal some path by which energy is added quietly, perhaps by the evaporation of water, or some change of temperature—both of them forces driven ultimately by the Sun.

to a formula Einstein developed in another of his 1905 papers: $E=mc^2$. In this formula, E is the energy from the complete transformation into energy of some bit of matter whose rest mass is m. How big is this energy? The c^2 gives the amount, since c is the famous speed of light in a vacuum, a big number, and the square of such a big number is very big indeed. Even a nuclear bomb or power plant manages to convert only a little of its fuel's mass into energy, yet that little bit can power—or destroy—whole cities.

Black Holes. This theory also allows for the possibility of black holes. After stars use up their nuclear fuel and cease emitting light, they may become condensed objects that create strong gravitational fields. They are theorized to have such a strong gravitational pull that not even light can escape. If light or any object comes in contact with the collapsed star, it is drawn in and cannot escape. Black holes are thought to look like black regions of space that can grow larger by sucking in matter, such as other stars. According to physicists, black holes can, however, be detected by X-ray emissions, though these are not X-rays emitted from inside the hole itself. Instead, the space gas pulled into the hole's gravitation field becomes superheated and emits X-rays on its way down into the hole. Thus, the invisible object can be guessed at from the X-rays around it. Some scientists believe that several X-ray emissions detected in the Milky Way are emanating from black holes. It has been suggested that the star Cygnus-1 may one day be confirmed to be a black hole.

Sources

Hawking, Stephen W. *A Brief History of Time.* New York: Bantam Books, 1988.

Schwartz, A. Truman, et al. *Chemistry in Context.* Dubuque, IA: Wm. C. Brown Publishers, 1994. ©American Chemical Society.

Van Doren, Charles. *A History of Knowledge.* New York: Carol Publishing Group, 1991.

Williams, Robert H. "Fuel Cells: The Clean Machine," *Technology Review* 97 (April 1994).

CHAPTER FOUR

Global Energy Use

From the time humans first made fire around 500,000 B.C., they have used energy to help them work. For most of our history, the energy we have used has come directly or indirectly from Earth's main source of energy—the Sun. The firewood we used for so many centuries came from trees that converted the Sun's energy into food that helped them grow. The fossil fuels we have relied on so heavily in recent years are the remains of plants and animals that lived millions of years ago. We have used these gifts from the Sun without much thought about the future, but if our way of life is to survive, we will have to find new fuels and more efficient ways of using the ones we have.

HUMANITY'S ABILITY TO HARNESS ENERGY

Early Humans. Early humans were nomadic hunters and gatherers who relied on primitive, hand-made tools to accomplish the basic tasks necessary for life. The ability to make fire allowed humans to cook food, make pottery, and provide themselves with warmth and light. As humans became better adapted to their environment, the advantages of living in larger, settled groups—safety and the sharing of food, resources, and responsibilities—became apparent.

Early civilizations, such as those found in the Tigris-Euphrates, Nile, and Huang Ho (Yellow River) valleys, focused on farming. Humans were beginning to exert more control over their environment. They harnessed the power of domestic animals to help them carry goods, plow fields, and develop irrigation systems. Many early civilizations also exploited the power of other human beings. Huge numbers of slaves or paid laborers built the Egyptian pyramids and the Roman aqueducts.

Modern Society's Use of Energy. As humans expanded their sources of energy, societies became more advanced. Better tools and improved farming methods led to increased agricultural production. Cities could develop now that people in the villages did not have to devote all their energy to farming. As civilization became more complex, humans expanded their expectations and desires, life expectancy increased, and world population grew, as did the need for energy. Today we need great amounts of energy to maintain our standard of living.

Transportation. Carrying people and goods from one place to another requires a network of transportation facilities. In the past, people provided

Our ancestors had access to limited forms of energy, but their accomplishments were tremendous.

for most of their own needs locally. Today, railroads, trucks, and, to a lesser extent, airplanes deliver goods across the country and around the world. In a similar way, personal automobiles have become a necessity. Our transportation needs consume great quantities of petroleum in the form of gasoline, diesel fuel, and jet fuel. Factories that process our food, make our clothing, and produce many other of life's necessities require vast amounts of fossil fuels to power their generators, as do the power plants that provide electricity to homes and businesses.

Wasting Energy. It is also important to keep in mind that the process of energy conversion involves a substantial amount of waste. Whether it's the waste heat that escapes from fossil fuel and nuclear power plants or the natural gas that escapes when drilling for oil, we are not using our available resources as efficiently as we can. Throughout human history, the amount of energy consumed has

grown steadily. The need for energy will continue to grow, as will the need to find new sources and more efficient ways of using them.

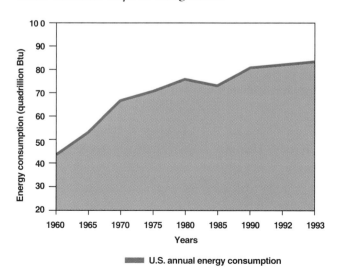

The United States uses more energy each year, as shown by Department of Energy annual reviews.

When traffic stalls on a highway, like this one near the French-Italian border, the many idling motors of the nonmoving vehicles represent a tremendous waste of fuel. This is a mileage of zero miles per gallon.

BIOMASS

The term *biomass* is an abbreviation for biological mass, a scientific term that means the total amount of living material provided by a given area. Biomass energy comes from biological products such as fuelwood, crop residues, and dung. When early humans discovered the advantages of fire, they were relying on biomass. Wood, bark, and other forms of vegetation were burned to provide heat for warmth and cooking. The use of biomass allowed early people to deal with cold and hunger.

Biomass, in the form of wood or other burnable items, is basically stored solar energy. Through the process of photosynthesis, energy from the Sun is absorbed and used by vegetation. As the plant grows, more energy is absorbed and stored in the leaves, stem, trunk, and root system. When the plant or tree is cut down for use as fuel, photosynthesis stops, but the energy collected over the plant's life is stored within its cells. By burning the fuel, the energy that was captured and stored by the plant is released, creating heat and light.

From prehistoric times through the late 18th century, biomass in the form of wood was the world's primary source of fuel. Local supplies of wood provided fuel for heating, cooking, and small industrial enterprises such as making metal tools. By the 18th century, England and many other Old World countries were running out of firewood. Forests had been stripped bare for fuel or farmland. By that time, however, another bountiful resource was available—coal.

Today, biomass is still the dominant source of fuel in many parts of Asia and Africa. In the early 1990s, it was estimated that about 75% of the energy from biomass was produced in developing countries, where wood is used for fuel, charcoal is burned, and dung is used in stoves. Biomass is easily available, although supplies vary greatly from country to country. In countries like Nepal and Malawi, biomass constitutes more than 90% of total energy use. Wood and dung have been used for centuries as sources of heating and fuel in many countries. The main advantage of biomass is that it can be used directly as a fuel to produce heat on a local level.

Disadvantages and Environmental Impact of Biomass. The disadvantages of traditional uses of biomass have become clear over the centuries. Solid biomass, such as wood or trash, has a low energy content per unit of weight. In other words, it takes a great deal of wood to produce the same amount of heat that can be produced by oil or coal. This leads to a second problem: biomass must be collected over a wide area to get the amounts needed to fulfill the demand. In many places, forests have been stripped bare through the harvesting of biomass. Transportation and handling becomes a major factor in communities that depend on wood for heating. Biomass systems are also inefficient, resulting in more waste products that create air pollution. Biomass fuels release carbon dioxide (CO_2) when burned, and the amount of CO_2 released is equal to the amount extracted from the atmosphere during the period of growth.

Future of Biomass. In industrialized countries, biomass is considered a renewable energy source that holds promise for future energy generation. The principal suggested use of biomass technology is not in cooking or heating but in the production of ethanol, a kind of alcohol that can be used as a clean-burning fuel for automobiles. Ethanol is produced mainly from corn and other agricultural products and sometimes from trees. Technology for the production of this fuel is still evolving.

WIND, WATER, AND GAS

While the Sun enables plants to grow and produce wood for fuel, it also provided other sources of energy for ancient people. The Sun unevenly heats the air surrounding Earth, creating wind. The Egyptians, who were sailing boats along the Nile by 3000 B.C., were probably the first to make use of this great wind power. Sailing ships continued to be the main means of transporting people and goods over the sea until the 19th century.

Wind Energy. Windmills first appeared around the 7th century A.D. in Persia (now known as Iran), where they were used for grinding grain and lifting water. Windmills also became popular in many parts of Europe, where as early as the 12th century they pumped water for irrigation and drinking. Famous for its windmills in more modern times is the Netherlands, where more than 20,000 were used in the 18th centu-

ry to pump water from low-lying land. In the United States, farmers used windmills to pump water and to generate electricity well into the 20th century. Wind farms, or fields of windmills, have also been used on a larger scale to generate electricity in Europe and the United States. However, the availability of cheap fossil fuels to produce electricity has reduced the economic incentive for wind-generated power.

ENVIROBIT

Biomass was the first energy source harnessed for human use. Only in the past 100 years have fossil fuels replaced wood as the primary fuel.

Water Energy. In many ways, water could be considered another gift from the Sun in that the Sun's energy fuels the hydrologic cycle—the endless circulation of Earth's water from the oceans, to the clouds, to rivers and streams, and back to the ocean. The power of running water has been exploited since ancient times. Greek historians documented the use of water wheels in the 1st century B.C., while the Roman Empire made great use of water-powered mills. These mills converted the kinetic energy of flowing water to mechanical energy to grind corn and other grains.

In more recent times, people have been interested in converting the energy of flowing water into electric power. Rushing water passes through turbines and generators to produce electricity. In some countries, such as Norway and Nepal, where geography and topography have made this resource available, hydroelectric plants produce most of the electricity. Hydroelectric plants are costly, both in dollars and in their effect on the land around them. In many countries, the supply of water power is not located near the demand, requiring long transmission lines. Many more potential hydropower sites are available and may yet be developed, but every source of energy has its cost, and the dams that back the water up can also flood farmlands and forests.

This windmill "farm" in San Jacinto, California, takes advantage of strong winds flowing over barren slopes. As the blades turn, electricity is generated.

The hydroelectric plant at Itaipu Dam generates electricity for Brazil.

Natural Gas. Like wind and water, natural gas is a resource with a long history of human use. The Chinese reportedly used natural gas in the 3rd century A.D. to help produce salt. They piped the gas through hollow bamboo to containers of salt water. When the gas was burned, the water evaporated and salt was left behind. Natural gas was used for lighting buildings in England and the United States in the early 1800s. There were many dangers associated with its use, however. Until new pipes were invented, fires and explosions occurred frequently.

Natural gas was formed in the same way as petroleum—from the remains of ancient plants and animals—and is frequently found in the same formations as petroleum. Natural gas burns more cleanly than coal and oil and is not subject to spillage. Once its advantages became apparent, great networks of pipelines were built to carry the gas from the well to the consumer. A negative effect of natural gas is how it is transported. These pipelines have disrupted migration patterns of certain terrestrial wildlife, such as caribou. The use of natural gas has increased steadily in the 20th century. But as with other fossil fuels, supplies of this popular fuel will not last forever.

FOSSIL FUELS

Like natural gas, coal and oil are fossil fuels that formed from the remains of plants and animals that were buried under layers of rock several hundred million years ago. Time, pressure, and heat gradually turned the dead plants and animals into coal, oil, and natural gas. Like water and wind, fossil fuels also came indirectly from the Sun. In a process called photosynthesis, energy from the Sun, along with water and carbon dioxide, made it possible for the plants to grow and make their own food millions of years ago. The animals that ate the plants got energy from them. When the plants and animals died, the energy from the Sun was stored in their bodies. Today, when we use fossil fuels, we are using this stored sunshine.

Fossil fuels are found in many different places in the world. Heat from within the Earth creates the conditions to turn underground plant material into oil and gas. Fossil fuels collect in pools or in the cracks and pores of underground rocks. Many supplies of oil can be found under the ocean floor in sediment. Some pools of oil are very large, extending several hundred meters deep. Most of the oil that has been found underground is in large oil fields. The main concentrations of oil are in the Persian Gulf, North and West Africa, the Gulf of Mexico, and the North Sea.

People have used oil in many forms for thousands of years. Since ancient times, oil has been seeping from the ground (sometimes as asphalt or tar). The Chinese may have used petroleum as a fuel around 200 B.C. Asphalt, a thick form of oil, was used to pave roads in ancient times. Native Americans used oil for fuel and medicine. When heated, oil can be refined into kerosene, which was traditionally used for lamps. In the mid-1800s, when a shortage of whale oil (which is not related to oil found in the Earth) spurred a search for a substitute, people began to produce kerosene in larger quantities.

The search for more sources of oil began in the mid-19th century and continues to this day. When the first wells were dug, they extended about 20 meters (65 feet) into the ground. Today's oil wells may be 2 kilometers (1.24 miles) deep. This is just one more sign that Earth's supply of fossil fuels is not inexhaustible.

FINDING AND REFINING OIL

Edwin L. Drake (1819–1880) drilled the first oil well near Titusville, Pennsylvania, on August 27, 1859. While that particular well produced only a few barrels of oil a day, it was the first time that the fossil fuel had been extracted from its reservoir in the Earth. All the oil used earlier had been at the surface already, in seeps or pools. By the end of the century, wells near Titusville were producing

more than 30 million barrels of oil a year. Much of the oil from these early wells was refined, or purified, to make kerosene for lamps. Much was just thrown away, however, as no one had yet found much use for the heavier fractions of oil, the ones too thick to make easily into kerosene.

Exploration for oil depends on the knowledge of Earth's geology. After geologists look for signs of underground traps or pools where oil may have collected, exploratory wells are drilled into the Earth to confirm the presence of oil. Oil and gas wells are drilled using large steel pipes with a drill bit that breaks up rock. A mixture of materials called "mud" is piped down to the drill bit to lubricate it and create pressure, which keeps out the water. When the drill finds oil, a pipe is put in the hole to extract it. Pipes and valves are added to control the oil as it is withdrawn. Additional wells can be drilled in the same area to increase productivity.

Refining oil involves a distillation process. The petroleum, a complex mixture of chemicals commonly called fractions of the oil, is heated under pressure in a special furnace. The hot oil then moves to the bottom of a tall fractionating tower, where the pressure is released. The hot liquid turns to vapor, which rises up the tower. As the vapor rises, it cools and condenses. Different compounds in the petroleum condense at different temperatures and are collected in separate shelves of the tower. Among the products of the refining process are asphalt, lubricating oil, fuel oil, kerosene, and gasoline.

USES OF OIL

After the construction of Drake's first well, the oil industry quickly became a big business. In the United States, oil wells and refineries sprang up in Pennsylvania, Ohio, and other midwestern states; even richer deposits were discovered in Texas and Louisiana. However, these pale in comparison to the oil riches of the Middle East. The apparent abundance of oil, its cleanliness compared to coal, its versatility, and the relative ease with which it could be produced and transported guaranteed its role as a prime energy source. But it was almost a century

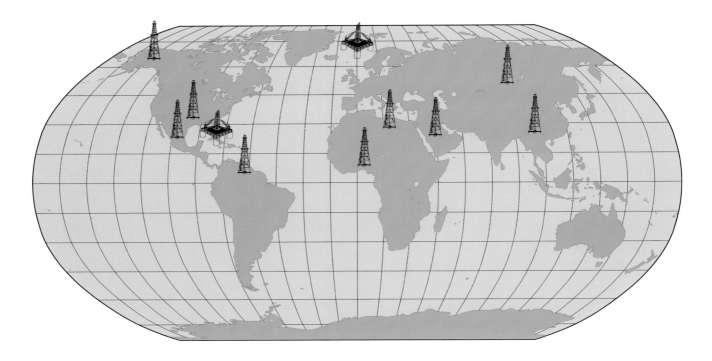

Each of these oil-rich areas of the world produces more than 3 million barrels of oil a day.

after Drake's strike in Titusville before the consumption of oil surpassed that of coal.

Perhaps the most significant reason for oil's dominance is the automobile. European and American scientists and inventors worked for years to turn their visions of self-propelled road vehicles into reality. In 1887, German engineer Gottlieb Daimler (1834-1900) achieved a breakthrough when he developed a high-speed, gasoline-powered, internal-combustion engine. In 1885, another German engineer, Karl Benz (1844-1929), produced a gasoline-powered tricycle. In the United States, Henry Ford (1863-1947) had his own visions. Around the turn of the century, he produced several experimental vehicles, as did many other budding entrepreneurs. But it was the development of Ford's assembly-line production system that made automobiles affordable. Cars became a necessary means of transportation, and to keep them moving, gasoline production skyrocketed.

More and more uses were found for petroleum and its by-products. By 1950, the United States had become an importer of oil because the domestic supply could no longer meet the demand. Huge oil reserves in the Middle East were now fueling most of the world's industrial nations. Hundreds of chemical products, called petrochemicals, are also made from oil, including plastics, synthetic rubber and fiber, drugs, fertilizers, synthetic detergents, explosives, insecticides, and dyes.

STEAM AND COMBUSTION

With the dawn of the Industrial Revolution, humankind entered a new era. Historians agree that the development of the first practical steam engine in the late 1700s sparked a revolution in the capacity of industry to produce—anything. Though the ancient Greeks and others had known the principle, the few actual steam machines they built were essentially toys or display pieces. The

The tall towers you see out in an oil field are the drilling rigs. The "roughnecks," as these workers are called, are hoping for a strike near Odessa, Texas. If they make their strike, the tower may be moved on to another drilling site, while a much shorter structure does the actual pumping.

new, powerful steam engine allowed humans, for the first time, to convert heat energy from fuel into useful work on a practical scale.

It was the search for better ways to mine coal that led to the steam engine. As miners picked their way along underground seams of coal, the mine shafts frequently flooded, and sometimes miners died. Existing pumps could not keep up with the inflow of water. In 1698, English engineer Thomas Savery (1650-1715) developed a "fire engine" that used fire to boil water, creating steam that powered a pump. Soon after, English inventor Thomas Newcomen (1663-1729) produced an improved steam engine. Water in the mines could now be pumped out faster than it flowed in. Coal mines could be dug deeper, allowing expanded production of this increasingly valuable resource.

In 1769, Scottish inventor James Watt (1736-1819) received a patent on a steam engine that operated even more efficiently. By the turn of the century, hun-

dreds had been sold not only to pump water but also to supply power to textile and grain mills. Unlike wind and water, the steam engine provided power at locations convenient to the user, not just beside rapidly flowing streams and rivers or on windy hilltops. Englishman Richard Trevithick (1771-1833) and American Oliver Evans (1755-1819), working independently, made even further improvements by building high-pressure steam engines. Until supplies dwindled, wood was the primary fuel for steam engines; thereafter, coal became a plentiful source. Powered by steam engines, factories could be built almost anywhere, and they were. This greatly increased the demand for coal.

Industrial development made rapid strides in the 1800s. In France, 600 steam engines were in operation in 1830; by 1847, there were more than 4,800. The steam engine also led to great advances in transportation. American engineer Robert Fulton

Henry Ford's Model T sparked the gasoline revolution. Here he stands in 1946 between his first 1892 car (right) and his company's ten-millionth (left).

(1765-1815) built what is considered the first successful steamboat, which sailed from New York City to Albany in 32 hours in August 1807. In Wales, Trevithick applied the power of steam to a locomotive, which was used to transport coal.

Despite the major progress that resulted from steam engines, they were still large and awkward to operate. The invention of the internal-combustion engine by Frenchman Jean Lenoir (1822-1900) around 1860 was another major breakthrough. Both the steam engine and the internal-combustion engine burn fuel to change heat energy into mechanical energy. However, the steam engine is an external-combustion engine, meaning it gets its energy from fuel burned outside the engine. In an internal-combustion engine, the fuel is burned inside. Besides being much more efficient, the internal-combustion engine weighed far less than the steam engine. And because gasoline has a higher energy content than the same amount of coal, much more power could be produced by the lightweight engine fueled by gasoline. Automobiles, and even airplanes, became a practical possibility.

THE IMPORTANCE OF COAL

History of Coal. As with the other fossil fuels, the formation of coal began some 300 million years ago. As dead plant material decayed in prehistoric swamps, layers of dirt and rock gradually covered and compressed it; under intense heat and pressure it became peat, and as these increased, lignite, or brown coal. Some of the coal became even more compacted, becoming bituminous, or soft, coal. And finally the energy-rich, hard anthracite coal was formed.

Humans have a long history of coal use: the Chinese used coal before 1000 B.C.; the Book of Proverbs in the Bible mentions coal; and Native Americans used coal in the process of making pottery. Coal later played an important role in fueling the Industrial Revolution. As steam engines were perfected, new and improved methods of mining coal became possible, which in turn made possible the production of more steam engines. Coal was not the primary fuel for steam engines until the end of

ENVIROBIT

Coal is the world's most abundant fossil-fuel energy source. It provides more than three times the energy supplied by oil and gas combined.

the 18th century, when wood supplies could no longer meet the demand for fuel. Europe's forests had been largely chopped down, either to provide firewood or to clear land for agriculture.

The development of the steam engine greatly improved coal-mining methods. The earliest users of coal had simply gathered it from outcroppings, places where the coal was exposed on the surface. Underground mines produced more coal, although it was still mined by primitive methods—miners using picks and other hand tools to dig it from the beds. With the help of ponies, mules, and other animals, the miners carried buckets and wheelbarrows full of coal to the surface. Later, mine cars with wheels were used, and humans or animals pulled the coal cars over wooden planks up the steep tunnels. The steam engine applied power to the mining process. Miners could dig deeper mines and locomotives could transport the coal faster and farther.

Mining. Since the Industrial Revolution, many methods of coal mining have been used, depending on the location and nature of the coal formation. If the coal is located near the surface, surface- or strip-mining methods are used. Giant earth-moving machines literally strip away the Earth's surface to get at the underlying coal seams. In most areas, the soil and other material that is removed is saved and put back once the coal has been extracted. Explosives are often used to break up the coal, which is then hauled away by huge trucks. Surface mining alters the landscape drastically, sometimes destroying farms and forests or hills and valleys. Erosion set off by soil removal frequently becomes a problem, made even worse by acid runoff from the exposed areas. But as people became more aware of the environmental damage caused by mining, laws were passed

This coal miner near Benton, Illinois, must work in the shelter of the hydraulic roof supports seen over his head. These supports travel with him, and with the great mining machine that chews through the coal in this "longwall" mining method. Behind the machine, the roof may simply be allowed to collapse as the coal is dug out beneath it.

and coal companies have worked hard to restore lands to their original condition.

Although strip mining has many disadvantages, it is far safer for the workers involved than underground mining, the other major method of extracting coal. Thousands of lives have been lost over the years from explosions and falling rock in underground mines. Black lung disease, caused by breathing coal dust, has also killed many miners. Even though laws have been enacted and methods of mining improved, many miners are still killed each year in coal mines around the world.

Several techniques are used in underground mining. Getting to the seam of coal is the first problem. If the coal is located near the surface of a hill, an opening may be made right into the seam. This is called a drift mine. Miners drill into the coal and follow the seam into the hillside. Coal cars or conveyor belts carry the coal out. If the coal is farther down, a slope may be excavated through the rock. Miners and machines travel through the tunnel to get to the coal, and again coal cars or conveyor belts transport the coal to the surface. For coal beds deep underground, a vertical shaft is built. Elevators large enough to carry miners and huge pieces of equipment are then installed in the shaft.

To extract the coal, most mines employ the room-and-pillar technique. Cutters excavate a series of rooms into the coal, leaving pillars of coal behind to support the mine roof. Machines called continuous miners take the coal from the seam and load it onto conveyor belts or shuttle cars that carry it out of the mine. A newer technique called longwall mining employs a huge cutting machine that scrapes back and forth across a seam of coal, which may be 250 meters (820 feet) long. The machine cuts and removes the coal in the same operation, and has its own roof supports that move along with it so that it does not need to leave pillars of valuable coal behind as supports.

The coal is cleaned, sorted, and graded above ground before being shipped via train, barge, or some other means of transportation to one of its many possible destinations. Coal is used in electric-power generation, making steel, and until the middle of the 20th century it was the main power source for industry throughout the world. Coal is the most abundant of the fossil fuels, although many problems are associated with its use.

Air Pollution. Coal is messy and difficult to transport because of its bulkiness. When burned, it pollutes the air with smoke, ash, sulfur and carbon dioxide, and a variety of other hazardous substances. As early as the late 1800s, thick, polluting fogs enveloped London, England, and other cities where coal was burned indiscriminately. During the 20th century, some countries, notably the United States, passed laws requiring companies to install scrubbers and other devices on smokestacks to remove at least some of the pollutants from coal emissions. But by the time the laws were passed, cleaner, more convenient sources of power had begun to displace coal.

ELECTRICITY

Electrical energy is the most versatile source of power. It can be produced in various ways and converted easily into many useful forms. Electricity can be converted to the light energy of a light bulb, the heat energy of a hair dryer, or the sound energy of a stereo receiver. Today, huge power plants in many parts of the world produce electricity that enables us to enjoy a life-style we could not have imagined 100 years ago.

The word *electricity* comes from the Greek word *electron*, meaning "amber." Philosophers in ancient Greece recognized that when amber was rubbed, it could attract lightweight objects. Many centuries would pass before scientists began to understand the nature of this phenomenon. In the 17th and 18th centuries, scientists found other ways of producing electric charges and other materials that had the same characteristics as amber.

American inventor and statesman Benjamin Franklin (1706–1790) experimented with electricity in the mid-1700s. With his famous lightning and kite experiment, he proved that lightning is electricity. At the time, Franklin theorized that electricity was some sort of fluid. Today, we know that electricity comes from the movement of electrons, negatively charged particles that move rapidly around an atom's nucleus. Electrons can be freed from atoms and moved through certain substances called conductors. The electrons moving through a conductor, such as a wire, produce an electric current.

Around 1800, an Italian professor named Alessandro Volta (1745-1827) invented what was soon called a voltaic pile, a stack of metal disks separated by moist paper. This became the first "battery" to produce a steady stream of electric current. Electrons flowing in the same direction in a wire produce what is called direct current (DC). But electrons can move in both directions along a wire, producing what is called alternating current (AC). Electric current flows along closed, continuous paths called circuits. To keep the current moving, the source of electrons must have different charges at each end of the wire. One end must have a negative charge, and the other a positive charge. The difference in the charges is called the potential difference, or voltage, the amount of energy available to move charges along the wire from one end toward the other. Voltage is measured in units called volts.

Resistance opposes the flow of electric currents. The length, thickness, and composition of the wire as well as temperature all affect resistance. Electrical resistance is measured in units called ohms. The rate at which electric current flows through a wire is measured in amperes. The greater the number of electrons flowing past a particular point in a circuit, the greater the number of amps.

Transportation of Electricity. Electric power is the rate at which electricity does work or provides energy. Power that enters a home is measured in units called watts, which were named after the steam engine pioneer James Watt. One thousand watts is called a kilowatt. A kilowatt-hour is the amount of energy used to produce 1,000 watts (or about 10 light bulbs rated 100 watts) for one hour. Most households and businesses measure their energy use in kilowatt-hours.

In 1820, Danish scientist Hans Christian Oersted (1777-1851) discovered that an electric current attracted a magnet; in other words, electricity could produce magnetism. Two other scientists, Joseph Henry (1797-1878) in the United States and Michael Faraday (1791-1867) in England, independently explored the possibility that magnetism could produce electricity. They each experimented by moving a magnet in and out of a wire coil.

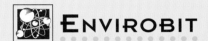

ENVIROBIT

The United States, with only 5% of the world's population, uses about 25% of the total energy produced each year.

Current flowed through the coil, and as long as the magnet kept moving, the current continued to flow. This process, called electromagnetic induction, allows generators to make electric power and transformers to change voltage and current as they travel to different locations.

Electricity is unique in that it is instantly available as soon as it is produced. Energy generated by electric power plants cannot be stored. It travels along wires, called transmission lines, from the producer to customers. The earliest transmission systems were simple networks of overhead wires. But as cities grew and the number of connections increased, the transmission systems have become increasingly complex. Overhead wires are still common in many communities, although some cities and urban areas have installed underground cables to carry large amounts of electricity in densely populated areas. Because voltage is always lost over long distances, electric power plants convert electricity to high-voltage power, which can be carried for thousands of kilometers (miles) on overhead cables with less loss than with lower voltages. These networks carry up to 765,000 volts. Power companies then use substations to reduce the voltage to 12,500 to 138,000 volts, which is used in industries, electric rail systems, and subways. Voltage is further reduced and distributed to smaller industries at 2,000 to 34,000 volts. The network extends to streetlights and traffic signals and is finally reduced to 110 or 220 volts before it is wired into homes and small businesses. Nearly all consumers of electric power in the United States and Europe use electricity at either 110 or 220 volts.

The complex web of an electric generating system is designed to meet the demand of most customers at peak periods. Private and public electric generating companies are interconnected with a network of high-voltage power lines that allows for flexibility in energy production. But demand for electricity can still place a great deal of stress on the system. With the advent of large-scale air conditioning, peak periods in the United States now occur on summer afternoons, when businesses and homes place the greatest demands on the electric system. Other peak periods include cold weather, when electric power is used to generate heat. Power-system managers must control the production and distribution system carefully to avoid surges and power blackouts. When a disruption to the system occurs, engineers may be able to restore service quickly by calling on other resources of the network. Natural disasters can traumatize the electric generating system. Since so much of the system is strung up on wires, the system is easily affected by storms and falling trees.

Revolutionary Development. Electricity opened up a world of possibilities. Soon after Thomas Edison (1847–1931) developed a long-lasting incandescent lamp in 1879, electric streetlights began replacing gas lamps in New York City and other American cities. Edison also spearheaded the building of a coal-burning power plant, the Pearl Street Power Station in New York. When the station began producing electricity in 1882, it served 60 customers. The development of street lighting and household electricity created a revolution in the way people lived. City lights allowed virtually all of the daily functions of home and business to continue at night.

In German cities, the electric streetcar made its appearance by 1881. Elevated electric trains began operating in the U.S. cities of Chicago, Boston, and New York by the early 1900s. High-speed electric railways continue to operate in many European countries and Japan. Electricity has revolutionized many other aspects of modern life as well. The number of electric power plants grew rapidly in the late 1800s and early 20th century. In the 1930s, U.S. president Franklin D. Roosevelt's Rural Electrification Administration was established to bring electricity to wide expanses of rural areas in the United States.

As more and more homes and businesses were connected, more and more labor-saving devices were invented, including the telephone, the telegraph, the automatic milking machine, and the vacuum cleaner. The list goes on and, in fact, continues to be expanded today. In American homes, for example, where 40 years ago one television set was a rarity, residents may now have one set in each room, complete with a wide screen and speakers. Personal computers are also found in increasing numbers of homes, demonstrating that what was once a luxury item may now be considered a necessity.

Growing demand puts a considerable burden on electric utilities. Fossil fuels are becoming increasingly expensive. Some people propose relying more on nuclear power as an alternative source of energy. The quest for possible sites for hydroelectric stations has also been renewed, but many of the best locations for dams and reservoirs have already been used. The search for new ways to produce electricity continues as well.

Environmental Effects. Electricity is clean in its final use, but the fuels and other power sources used to produce it have harmful effects on the environment. Air pollution caused by the burning of fossil fuels continues to be a problem. If nuclear energy is pursued, safety issues and questions regarding nuclear waste must be addressed. The environment is invariably altered when hydroelectric plants are built or fossil fuels are mined. Thermal pollution, caused primarily by waste heat from power plants, is an ever-present problem.

The cost of building new power plants to meet peak demand has become prohibitive in many areas. In addition, environmental concerns about pollution problems caused by burning coal or producing nuclear power has led to programs to conserve electricity by reducing peak demand and implementing innovative energy-conservation ideas. Some power companies now offer incentives to encourage the replacement of electrical lighting and heating systems to increase efficiency. Instead of building new plants, these companies encourage the use of insulation, energy-conserving light bulbs, and off-peak use of energy. A relatively simple change from incandescent to fluorescent lighting can reduce household demand by 30% to 40%. Multiplied by millions of homes and businesses, the savings could be enough to offset the need for new power plants.

NUCLEAR POWER

Nuclear power plants produce electric power in much the same way that fossil-fuel–burning plants do. They heat water to make steam, which turns the blades of a turbine, causing a generator to produce electricity. But in nuclear plants, heat is generated by the fission, or splitting, of the nuclei of uranium atoms.

The Dawn of the Nuclear Age. The nuclear age began with the explosion of atomic bombs in Hiroshima and Nagasaki in 1945. These bombs unleashed incredible power. The demand for electricity was growing rapidly, and governments and scientists were searching for new ways to produce it. Even in the 1950s, people realized that our supply of fossil fuels would not last forever. To many, nuclear energy seemed to be the solution. Albert Einstein's theory of relativity, first published in 1905, proposed that energy and matter were essentially different forms of the same thing. And according to his famous equation, $E=mc^2$, a little mass could equal a lot of energy.

When the nuclei of uranium atoms are split, energy and neutrons are released. The freed neutrons strike and split other uranium atoms, creating a chain reaction that releases tremendous amounts of energy. In atomic bombs used in World War II, the chain reaction was uncontrolled and the explosions produced temperatures of millions of degrees—the amount of energy equivalent to 18,200 metric tons (20,000 U.S. Tons) of TNT.

In a nuclear reactor, the chain reaction is carefully controlled. Different materials and methods are used to control the reaction. A reactor chamber may be more than 12 meters (40 feet) high with thick steel walls. Fuel in the form of uranium pellets is packed into tubes called fuel rods. Bundles of the rods are lowered into the chamber where water circulates around them. The water prevents the reactor from overheating and removes the heat to be used for power generation. Rods of cadmium or other neutron-absorbing substances are also inserted as control rods. Both the water and the control rods serve to slow down the neutrons, controlling the amount of heat energy produced. The heat energy is used to turn water into steam, which drives a turbine that generates electricity.

In 1957, when the first commercial nuclear reactor began producing electric power in the U.S. city of Shippingport, Pennsylvania, many hailed it as the beginning of a new era. Nuclear plants burned much more cleanly and efficiently than the traditional fossil-fuel–burning plants. But the development of nuclear power encountered obstacles from the beginning. Construction costs for the plants were

ENVIROBIT

A 0.45-kilogram (1 pound) pellet of enriched uranium contains nearly 3 million times the energy in a pound of coal.

much higher than originally estimated, and meeting government-imposed safety requirements added still more to the cost. In addition, citizen opposition to planned nuclear plants forced utilities to evaluate the pros and cons of nuclear energy before choosing it as an option. There are several reasons for concern.

The "atomic era," or "nuclear age," is dated by some from the first use of atomic bombs in warfare, in 1945. From an environmental point of view, a better date might be the first successsful nuclear reactor, in 1942. This was the key to the peaceful use of nuclear energy.

Environmental and Human Effects. Uranium is one of the few elements that is naturally radioactive. Its unstable isotopes gain stability by emitting radiation, which, although it cannot be seen or felt, can be extremely harmful to workers in uranium mines and mills who are exposed to uranium dust and radioactive gases. At the mills, usable uranium is extracted from ore, then crushed and ground into uranium concentrate called yellowcake. This process creates tremendous amounts of waste, called tailings, which are also highly radioactive. The uranium goes through an enrichment process, a sophisticated procedure that increases the concentration of the isotope U-235, the isotope of uranium that is fissionable. Once enriched, the uranium is changed into 1.27-centimeter (0.5-inch) uranium dioxide pellets and sealed in metal tubes. These tubes, or fuel rods, are mounted in bundles called fuel assemblies, which are loaded into the reactor. In most instances, remote-control devices handle the radioactive substances. Nonetheless, workers at the enrichment plants can be exposed to the hazards of radioactivity.

Despite all the precautions that are taken, the operation of any nuclear plant allows little margin for error. The familiar domes of nuclear power plants are actually thick concrete containment buildings. The reactor itself is placed inside a thick-walled reactor vessel. Water circulates throughout the reactor vessel to keep the reactor from overheating. Backup cooling systems are readily available. The uranium fuel itself is not enriched enough to produce an explosion. Should the cooling systems stop operating, the possibility of overheating to the point of a meltdown does exist.

This is what happened in April 1986 at Chernobyl in Ukraine, then part of the Soviet Union. No one knows exactly how it happened, but the reactor core overheated and melted, resulting in an explosion that blew the top off the reactor. Radioactive materials blasted more than 1.2 kilometers (0.75 mile) into the air and were spread by the winds. Fire burned for 10 days, allowing still more radioactivity to escape into the atmosphere. Clouds of radioactivity were detected across the globe, and a large area around the plant remains uninhabitable. The long-term effects of exposure to the radiation may not be known for decades, but the disaster brought public concern to a new level.

Enthusiasm for nuclear power had waned long before the accident at Chernobyl. The Arab oil embargo in 1973 actually served to curb the insatiable appetite for energy that had consumed many nations. Concerns over the health risks posed by nuclear energy inflated the costs of building new plants. A 1979 accident at the Three Mile Island nuclear plant in Middletown, Pennsylvania, heightened public fear. Orders for new plants were canceled, not only in the United States but in many countries around the world.

Many questions about nuclear power remain. In some parts of the world, where few other options are available, confidence has not been shaken. Many countries do not have large fossil-fuel resources and have not yet found ways to tap solar and other nonfossil-energy sources. In eastern Europe, for example, the need for electric power is so great that many nuclear plants with the same flawed design of the Chernobyl reactor continue to operate. The economies of these countries would simply shut down if their nuclear power plants stopped operating before some alternative was in place.

Disposal. Even if all nuclear plants were to cease operations this year, one problem would remain for years, even centuries, to come: what is to be done with the nuclear waste? The search for solutions to this problem has been going on for quite some time, but satisfactory solutions remain elusive. The nuclear process results in several kinds of radioactive waste. Low-level waste includes those materials used in the normal maintenance of the power plant. Rags, mops, clothing, protective boots and gloves are not highly

ENVIROBIT

Since 1900, the use of energy has nearly doubled every 20 years.

The 1986 Chernobyl nuclear plant explosion in Ukraine prompted an increased awareness of the potential risks and dangers of nuclear power.

radioactive, but they must be disposed of carefully. They are usually packed in drums and then shipped to low-level waste repositories where they are buried in trenches. Evidence exists that these methods may not be sufficient to protect the air, soil, and water, particularly with higher-level waste. For example, at Hanford Nuclear Reservation in Washington, buried barrels leaked nuclear waste which contaminated soil and groundwater. More precautions may need to be taken, such as burial in deep rock formations. Which localities will volunteer to be the site for nuclear-waste disposal has been a hotly debated political as well as environmental issue.

An even more serious question involves what to do with the spent fuel that can no longer sustain a chain reaction but still has enough radioactivity left to last for a long time. It may take several hundred thousand years before some nuclear waste has decayed to the point where it is no longer harmful. No one knows if there are underground rock formations that will be safe for that long. Currently, most spent fuel is kept in pools of water at reactor sites, a temporary and potentially hazardous situation. Some have proposed reprocessing the spent fuel. This procedure is extremely expensive and produces plutonium, a radioactive element that can only be used in weapons and breeder reactors.

Another issue that must be considered is what to do with nuclear plants that are no longer operating. Nuclear power plants are designed to operate for a limited number of years. The pioneering plant at Shippingport was the first plant to cease operation.

This particular plant was dismantled and shipped away at a tremendous expense. But other avenues for disposal are also being pursued, as questions remain as to how decommissioned plants should be sealed off and secured. One possibility is entombment, a process that leaves the plant in place but essentially buries it in concrete or other materials. It is currently being attempted at Chernobyl, with questionable results and potential health threats.

Questions and concerns remain about nuclear energy. By the same token, many questions remain as to how we will satisfy our energy needs once Earth's fossil fuels run out.

Sources

Clark, Wilson. *Energy for Survival: The Alternative to Extinction*. Garden City, NY: Anchor Press, 1974.

Golob, Richard, and Eric Brus. *The Almanac of Renewable Energy*. New York: Henry Holt, World Information Systems, 1993.

National Coal Association. *Facts About Coal—1990*. Washington, DC: 1990.

Nebel, Bernard J. *Environmental Science: The Way the World Works*. 2nd ed. Englewood Cliffs, NJ: Prentice-Hall, 1987.

Schwartz, A. Truman, et al. *Chemistry in Context: Applying Chemistry to Society*. Dubuque, IA: Wm. C. Brown Publishers, 1994.

World Energy Council. *Energy for Tomorrow's World*. New York: St. Martin's Press, 1993.

CHAPTER FIVE

Human Dependence on Energy

Energy is defined as the ability to do work. Humans get energy from food, enabling their bodies to function. In modern times, humans have come to rely on many external sources of energy to help them with their work. Our modern way of life has become dependent on these external sources of energy, particularly on nonrenewable supplies of coal, oil, and natural gas. A series of crises in recent years made us aware of our dependence. Growing concern about the impact of energy generation on the environment has caused us to reexamine the production and burning of fossil fuels. In the future, political conflicts and environmental concerns will greatly affect the cost of energy and the way we use it.

Uses of Energy. Over the past century, as our supplies of energy have diversified, so have the ways we make use of it. Almost every generation has developed new tools and devices to make life easier. What was an innovation or a rarity for one generation became a necessity for the next—cars, washing machines, televisions, and computers are just a few examples.

Reliance on Energy. In order to produce this expanding list of necessities, new and larger facto-ries requiring even more energy had to be built. Today, industrial production uses about one-quarter of the energy consumed in the United States. Whether producing steel, fertilizer, fabric, refrigerators, tractors, or jeans, U.S. factories require large amounts of coal, oil, and natural gas to function.

These same fossil fuels also provide the energy to heat virtually every building in the country. While our ancestors gathered around a fireplace to get warm, we are now accustomed to the comfort of heat throughout our homes, offices, stores, and factories. In some all-electric homes, electricity supplies the energy for heating as well as for cooling, lighting, and cooking. Electric power can be generated by fossil-fuel–burning plants, nuclear plants, or hydroelectric plants, plus small but growing amounts of power from modern wind turbines, geothermal stations, and other alternative sources under development. Electricity is produced in many ways and has a multitude of uses. Even if we get our heat from an oil burner or a natural-gas furnace, electric power almost certainly lights our homes. Electricity lights our factories and cities as well, and operates appli-

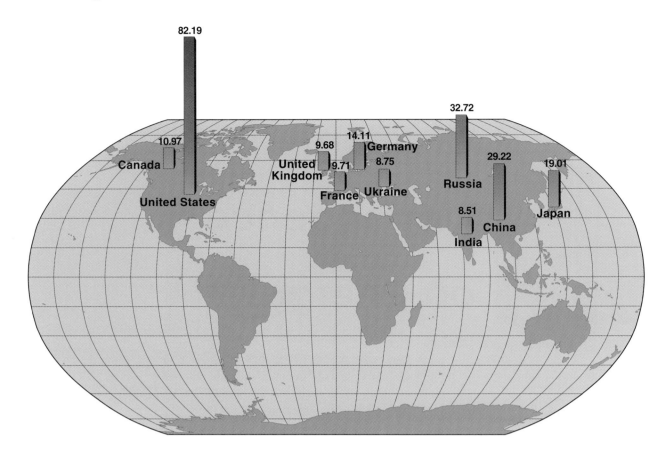

The United States, Russia, and China lead the world's top 10 energy-consuming nations.

ances and machines in homes and businesses. A brief power failure caused by a sudden thunderstorm can serve as a reminder of how much our lives depend on electricity.

Pervasive as electricity is, there is one area where it plays only a minor role—transportation. Our various means of transportation do, however, require great amounts of energy, particularly oil. Transportation needs consume more than half of all the oil used in the United States, mostly in the form of gasoline for passenger cars. Higher prices for gasoline, fuel-efficient cars, and other conservation measures have somewhat slowed the rate of increase in demand, but the automobile is still a tremendous energy user. In addition, society has become dependent on trucks, trains, and ships to carry goods across every nation and around the world.

In recent years, the need to transmit informa-

tion from place to place has created an even greater demand for energy. Local newspapers and letters sent through the postal system have been supplemented by television, radio, computers, facsimile (fax) machines, and overnight delivery services. Modern society has become used to instant access to information provided by a vast network of energy-consuming industries.

As the cost of energy increased, we developed a greater awareness of how dependent we had become on the availability of energy. We also realized that we could not continue to consume energy without any thought of the future. We began to think about more fuel-efficient cars and about adjusting the thermostats in our homes. Planners of office buildings began to think about more energy-efficient designs. At the same time, many lesser-developed countries (LDCs) are seeking their share of Earth's limited resources to improve their standard of living as well. Whatever country we live in, we need to consider where our energy will come from in the future.

DEPENDENCE ON THE AUTOMOBILE

Before Henry Ford's (1863-1947) affordable Model-Ts were introduced in 1908 and began rolling off the new moving assembly line in 1913, riding in a car was much like a sporting event. People may have driven around to show off on a Sunday afternoon or had races to see who could go faster than 32 kilometers per hour (20 miles per hour). Brave souls may have attempted cross-country treks, but given the reliability of the machines and the condition of the roads, most people did not venture more than a few kilometers (miles) from home. That situation did not last for long. While Henry Ford was producing millions of his basic black "Tin Lizzies," other manufacturers introduced new, more luxurious models that came in a variety of colors. Advertisements proclaimed the rewards of owning a car as well as the advantages of one model over another. The ads seemed to work. In 1920, 1 out of every 13 people in the United States was a registered car-owner. By 1930, that figure jumped to almost 1 out of every 6. Today, many families have two cars, or even more.

Henry Ford's early experimental cars of the 1890s led to the first mass-produced automobiles, starting in 1913.

The automobile has altered modern life. Before the advent of the car, most people lived in cities where they could walk from their homes to schools, to work, and to stores. As more people acquired cars, more roads were paved. During the Great Depression of the 1930s, the government put many citizens to work building a nationwide highway system. City dwellers could escape the increasing congestion of urban areas and settle in the suburbs, knowing they could rely on their cars to get them to work back in the city. Stores and other services followed them to the suburbs, as did jobs. Factories and office complexes were built farther away from the city centers. This enabled people to move even farther out and to become still more reliant on their cars.

The economies of many other nations, too, have come to rely on the automobile. A large network of industries supports the auto enterprise. Besides the multitude of businesses associated with the petroleum industry, many factories are involved in producing steel, rubber, glass, and other raw materials for the automobile. In addition, many people are employed in industries that depend indirectly on the automobile. Restaurants, hotels, and other recreational facilities depend on our ability to get there—most likely by car.

The cars that gave us freedom have, in some ways, made us more dependent as well. Many of us can no longer walk from home to school, or work, or the store. The sprawl of suburbia has made this nearly impossible; distances are simply too great. And while public transportation can solve some of these problems, it will not likely reduce our dependence on the automobile by much.

ENVIROBIT

In 1991, there was one car for every 1.7 residents in the United States. In China, there was one car for every 680 residents.

ENERGY AND DEVELOPING NATIONS

Industrialized Nations. Industrialized countries today consume a large portion of the world's energy resources. It is estimated that about half of the people in the world do not have access to commercial energy supplies. Instead of electricity, cars, and industrial machines, they rely on their own muscles, animal power, and traditional fuels such as wood. Their lives are similar in many ways to those of Europeans and Americans before the Industrial Revolution. The course of history since the Industrial Revolution has demonstrated that as countries develop technologi-

ENVIROBIT

World population is expected to increase to more than 8 billion by the year 2020. Most of the increase is expected in Asia and Africa.

cally, their populations grow and they consume increasing amounts of energy. Eventually, as has happened in the late 20th century in Europe, North America, and Japan, the rates of increase will level off.

In many nations, such as Tanzania in Africa, energy sources for cooking are largely limited to biomass such as wood and vegetation.

Lesser-Developed Countries. This pattern raises serious questions about future energy demand. Many nations have not developed what would be considered modern living standards. Yet many of these lesser-developed countries (LDCs) already have exceedingly large populations. While industrialized countries continue to use more energy, the demand for energy in developing countries is growing at a much faster rate, mainly because of population increases. As LDCs advance technologically, questions remain as to where they will get the energy to support these advances.

The problem is made even more complex by the fact that energy resources are not distributed evenly around the world. For example, some 70% of the world's known oil resources are found in the Middle East and North Africa. Nearly 90% of the total natural-gas reserves are known to be located in the former Soviet Union and the Middle East. Coal, too, is far more abundant in certain regions of the world, particularly North America and the former Soviet Union. While some lesser-developed countries may have untapped or undiscovered resources, the fact remains that most of them will almost certainly depend on imports of fossil fuels to spark their progress. For many of these nations, the cost of such fuels may be prohibitively high, especially when the costs of trans-

ENVIROBIT

North America and western Europe consumed about 50% of all the electricity used worldwide in 1990.

porting them are added in. As supplies of fossil fuels decline, costs will go up. It will be more expensive to find and extract these resources. LDCs will have the most difficulty paying the higher prices, thus threatening their ability to modernize.

The need for more energy resources in lesser-developed countries is obvious. Statistics have shown that there is a direct relationship between the amount of energy consumed in a country and its gross national product (GNP), the value of all the goods and services produced by the people in the country. GNP is a good measure of a country's standard of living. Increased energy use has also been associated with increased life expectancy, lower infant mortality rates, and lower rates of illiteracy. Expanded availability of electricity will dramatically improve the quality of life for millions in lesser-developed nations. Most of these countries have fewer than 20 cars per thousand people, while some developed countries have more than 500 cars per thousand.

No matter how quickly LDCs pursue technological advances and economic growth, it is important that they make an effort to use energy efficiently. Industrialized countries can help lesser-developed countries avoid that period of wasteful, polluting energy consumption by sharing their experience and knowledge. The results of such international cooperation will include less pressure on decreasing supplies of fossil fuels and less global pollution.

THE IMPACT OF ENERGY GENERATION

From the time people first began to rely on energy sources other than themselves, their use of energy has had an impact on the environment. By chopping down trees for firewood, humans altered countless ecosystems. Many forests were completely destroyed as populations grew and the search for firewood became more intense. Smoke from prehistoric fires was the first air pollution produced by humans.

Air Pollution. As the use of coal increased during the 19th century, skies over many industrial cities were blackened. Despite the hazards of the smoke and soot, industry smokestacks were perceived as a sign of progress. But it did not take too long before the dangers of coal were recognized. Today we know that coal produces a long list of hazardous substances when it is burned, including sulfur dioxide (SO_2) and nitrogen oxides (NO_x), major contributors to acid rain, as well as carbon monoxide (CO), carbon dioxide (CO_2), and particulate matter. Concern over environmental problems associated with coal led many utilities and industries to switch to cleaner-burning oil and natural gas as early as the 1940s. While these fossil fuels also emit sulfur and nitrogen oxides when they are burned, the quantities are much smaller.

Link to the Greenhouse Effect. Another major concern associated with the burning of fossil fuels is a buildup of carbon dioxide in the atmosphere. According to studies, the levels of carbon dioxide in the atmosphere have increased slowly but steadily during the 20th century. This increase can be attributed not only to fossil-fuel combustion but also to the clearing of forests in many parts of the world. Through the process of photosynthesis, green plants use light energy from the Sun, carbon dioxide, and water to produce food. Fewer plants means less carbon dioxide is taken in and, thus, removed from the atmosphere. An excess of carbon dioxide in the atmosphere can lead to what scientists call the greenhouse effect. The Sun's heat becomes trapped in Earth's atmosphere by carbon dioxide and other gases. If the trend continues, it has been theorized that global temperatures could increase to disastrous levels. At a United Nations–sponsored conference held in Rio de Janeiro, Brazil, in 1992, government representatives from many nations agreed to limit carbon dioxide emissions in an effort to prevent or slow global warming. This was an important first step in dealing with a potential planetwide environmental threat.

Waste Heat. The burning of fossil fuels also creates both useful heat and waste heat. In electric power plants, fossil fuels are burned to boil water, thereby producing steam to drive turbines, making electricity. But much heat remains in the steam. As the steam is then cooled and condensed back into water, the waste heat may be discharged into the air through cooling towers or it may be discharged along with the water into a nearby river or lake.

Airborne emissions fly out of smokestacks only to move with air currents or fall back to Earth.

Warm waters near many power plants have severely damaged aquatic ecosystems, altering the natural habitats of plants and aquatic animals or creating unnatural conditions that might, for example, encourage fish to spawn at the wrong time of year.

Environmental Damage. In addition to the hazards associated with the burning of fossil fuels, the mining, production, and transport of these resources threaten the environment in many ways. Acid runoff from coal mines is very difficult to control. It can kill surrounding plant life and work its way into nearby lakes, streams, and rivers, destroying aquatic ecosystems. Surface mining of coal has drastically changed the landscape in many parts of the world. Even where reclamation of the land is enforced by law, serious erosion can occur before the landscape is fully restored.

The way petroleum is drilled and transported offers many opportunities to spill vast quantities of the liquid fuel. Restoring the environment after an oil spill is almost an impossible task. When the fires were burning in the oil fields of Kuwait, some environmentalists pointed out that even during normal oil-field operations, some 250,000 barrels of oil spill into the Persian Gulf every year. The situation is the same around the world—the Gulf Coast of the United

ENVIROBIT

The Swedish government estimates that more than 30,000 of its lakes have pH levels under 5.9, an acidity high enough to severely damage many aquatic plants and animals.

This surface-mining operation in Siberia, like similar operations in the United States, will completely transform the surface of the land. Recently passed laws in the United States often require mining companies to restore a surface as much as possible to its previous condition.

CASE STUDY: FIRE IN THE OIL FIELDS OF KUWAIT

In August 1990, Iraq invaded the small Middle East country of Kuwait, one of the world's major exporters of petroleum. Industrialized countries had long feared this possibility. One of their major supplies of oil, the lifeblood of their economies, was cut off. In February 1991, following a brief war, Kuwait was liberated by United Nations forces led by troops from the United States. As Iraqi soldiers fled north, they left burning in their wake more than half of Kuwait's 940 oil wells. Some 6 million barrels of oil were gushing from the wells each day. Most of the oil burned, sending a toxic stream of smoke into the air. Some just spurted out onto the desert floor, creating lakes of oil deep enough to row a boat in.

Firefighters and specialists from around the world came to help the Kuwaitis. The operations were extremely dangerous.

The desert winds would blow the flames and smoke in one direction and then almost instantly shift to another, threatening to engulf firefighters and their equipment. Even after the fire at a well was extinguished, the flow of oil had to be stopped. The only way to do this was for the rescuers to go right to the outlet in the midst of the scalding oil and insert devices that pumped mud down into the well. This halted the flow of oil so that caps could be installed.

It took the international teams nearly nine months to extinguish the fires and close off

Patrolling marines in Kuwait cross a landscape of oil-soaked sands and burning wells left behind as Iraqi forces retreated.

the wells. Before the last well was finally capped in November 1991, more than 420 million gallons of oil had spewed into the environment. Some 483 kilometers (300 miles) of Persian Gulf coastline were covered with thick mats of oil, creating an almost instant graveyard for thousands of birds and other wildlife. And as the smoke from the fires spread with the winds, more than 1,554 square kilometers (600 square miles) of the region were visited by poisonous clouds.

The oil-field fires in Kuwait were actually put out much more quickly than anyone thought they could be. Nevertheless, they were an economic and environmental disaster. Before the war and the fires, Kuwait was able to produce nearly 2 million barrels of oil a day. Its production facilities were largely destroyed by the Iraqis and had to be rebuilt. This was a relatively easy job, however, compared to the task of restoring the environment. Even as the fires were still burning, scientists were studying their effects. On the ground, lakes of

Oil fires in Kuwait blazed up to 1,649°C (3,000°F), shooting flames up to 122 meters (400 feet) and turning sand into glass.

oil had engulfed desert plants and animals and lured thousands of migratory birds to their deaths. Blackened sands covered the beaches of the Persian Gulf. Oil coated the surface waters and sank to the seafloor, suffocating and poisoning many bottom-dwelling marine creatures.

Airplanes equipped with air-quality measurement instruments flew through the plumes of smoke, measuring the sulfur compounds and other poisons pouring into the air. During one month of the most intense fires, sulfur dioxide (SO_2) in the skies over Kuwait was measured at 20,000 metric tons (22,000 tons) per day. (All U.S. electric utilities combined emit fewer than 40,000 metric tons [44,000 tons] in a day.) Most of the soot and oil droplets remained in the lower parts of the atmosphere and did not travel great distances from the fires. Raindrops quickly condensed around the particles and fell as an oily drizzle. But between March and June instruments carried on air balloons detected increases in sulfuric acid particles in the skies over the U.S. state of Wyoming. Scientists theorize that some of the poisons from the skies over Kuwait were transported, perhaps by a thunderstorm, high into the atmosphere. Jet-stream winds then carried the particles swiftly around the globe.

The handling or cleanup of radioactive materials such as thorium requires extreme care. The blue coveralls with breathing masks are nicknamed "moon suits." Without them, these workers would risk not only skin damage but long-term internal problems as they breathed in radioactive dust particles that could lodge in their lungs.

States, the North Sea, and Venezuela's shoreline. In the day-to-day process of drilling for oil and sending it through pipelines and tankers, thousands of liters leak into the environment. However, this is a drop in the bucket compared to one crash of a supertanker. The world has witnessed many such events. The spill from the *Exxon Valdez* in 1989 was the worst in U.S. history. More than 37.8 million liters (10 million gallons) of oil were spilled, washing up on Alaska's coastline. Despite desperate clean-up efforts, thousands of birds and otters were killed. The full extent of damage to the environment may never be known.

The environmental impact of fossil fuels has led some to advocate expanded use of nuclear power as a cleaner-burning alternative. While nuclear plants produce few emissions in normal operation, more waste heat is created with nuclear power. This is because low temperatures must be maintained to avoid damaging the nuclear reactor. Damage to a reactor, as evidenced by a nuclear meltdown at the Chernobyl nuclear plant in Ukraine in 1986, can have devastating effects on human health and the environment. In addition, no solutions have yet been developed for dealing with the radioactive waste that nuclear plants generate.

As fossil-fuel supplies dwindle, we may attempt to look for more, to venture farther, and to dig deeper. Companies and governments may head north to the Arctic, an environmentally fragile area, to search for oil. More pipelines could be built, similar to those that stretch across the tundra bringing oil from Prudhoe Bay in Alaska. Exploratory oil wells might be dug along more kilometers (miles) of the continental shelf, posing a threat to ocean ecosystems. An oil spill in one of these less explored and less exploited regions of the planet could present a serious environmental hazard.

IMPLICATIONS FOR THE FUTURE

After the oil crisis of 1973, many people in the industrialized world came to realize—some for the first time—that Earth's energy resources will not last forever. Dire predictions were made that oil supplies would run out around the year 2000 and that natur-

al gas would be depleted soon after that. Industries and individuals adopted conservation measures. Government programs promoted research into alternative fuels and renewable energy resources.

Some of these efforts have had lasting benefits—people have discovered ways to use energy more efficiently—but many efforts again lagged as the cost of oil dropped back. But the fact remains that fossil-fuel supplies are finite. They were formed in the Earth millions of years ago and are being used faster than natural processes could produce them even if conditions were the same. Even before supplies run out, they will become scarcer and almost certainly more expensive to bring to market. Cost may put them out of reach for some consumers, or cause spot shortages in certain regions even while the world as a whole is still supplied.

Estimates vary as to the amount of resources remaining. Some experts speak in terms of time—35 years of oil, 60 years of natural gas, and perhaps 200 years worth of coal. It is difficult to make such predictions because so many variables are involved. Will more efficient ways of using these fuels be developed? Will new supplies be found? Will greater demands be placed on these resources by developing countries? No one can be sure.

Geologists can make fairly accurate estimates about the quantities of oil, natural gas, and coal that remain at known sites. Geological data and exploration can determine, with reasonable accuracy, how much of these fuels can be recovered from particular sites using existing technology. These are called proven reserves. Most experts believe that fossil fuels will continue to supply the bulk of our energy needs well into the 21st century, although they also agree that costs will increase. As supplies decline, it will become more difficult and more expensive to extract these resources. It is unlikely that major new reserves will be found, but costly exploration will probably continue. Because so much of our oil and natural gas is located in politically unstable regions, political turmoil may affect availability and pricing. There is growing concern about environmental protection. In particular, as gas and oil reserves decline and we are forced to rely more on coal, the cost of pollution-control measures will escalate unless new ways are found to use the coal both cleanly and economically.

ENVIROBIT

Geologists estimate that as of 1991, there were about 1.5 trillion metric tons (1.65 trillion tons) of proven-coal reserves in the world, but only 135 million metric tons (148.5 million tons) of oil.

Options for the future are limited in some respects. In order to make nonrenewable fuels last as long as possible, we must use them as efficiently as possible. After the 1973 oil crisis, conservation measures, along with an economic decline, resulted in a decreased demand for energy. Forecasts for the near future improved somewhat. In the United States during the record-setting cold winter of 1994, governments and businesses were forced to shut down in order to prevent overloaded utilities from crashing. Although this was a temporary situation caused by unusual circumstances, it serves as a reminder of what the future may hold. We need to use Earth's reserves of fossil fuels efficiently while we search for new sources of energy to replace them.

Sources

"From Output Squeeze to 'Price Embargo,' " *Time* (January 7, 1974).

Golob, Richard, and Eric Brus. *The Almanac of Renewable Energy.* New York: Henry Holt, World Information Systems, 1993.

Nebel, Bernard J. *Environmental Science: The Way the World Works.* 2nd ed. Englewood Cliffs, NJ: Prentice-Hall, 1987.

"Persian Gulf Pollution: Assessing the Damage One Year Later," *National Geographic* (February 1992).

Siegel, Mark, et al., eds. *Energy: An Issue of the '90s.* Wylie, TX: Information Plus, 1989.

"Special Report on Energy," *National Geographic* (February 1981).

Statistical Abstract of the United States, 1993.

"The Persian Gulf: After the Storm," *National Geographic* (August 1991).

We Americans. Washington, DC: National Geographic Society, 1976.

World Energy Council. *Energy for Tomorrow's World.* New York: St. Martin's Press, 1993.

CHAPTER SIX

Pollution from Energy Consumption

The expanded use of energy over the past hundred years has consumed great quantities of Earth's natural resources. Energy consumption has damaged the planet by polluting its air, land, and water. The production of electricity contributes many pollutants to the atmosphere, as do our gasoline-powered automobiles. Bodies of water have become dumping grounds for many of our wastes. The products we use every day require great amounts of energy to manufacture. The manufacturing process itself adds more toxic chemicals to the pollution mix. Although individuals also add pollutants to the environment, they can take steps to combat pollution problems. By conserving energy and using products more wisely, people can reduce the demand for resources and, at the same time, protect the environment.

AIR POLLUTION

Air pollution can take many forms, be composed of different substances, and pose varying levels of danger. Earth's atmosphere is able to disperse some air pollution—the winds can blow some of it away. But as more fossil fuels are burned and more auto exhausts enter the air, dispersal becomes more difficult. Virtually all air pollution eventually settles back on Earth, where it can cause damage to soil and water. Air pollution can attack certain materials, produce undesirable odors, and reduce visibility. Whether it is an inadvertent leak of radioactivity from a nuclear plant or smoke from a coal-burning power plant, air pollution threatens not only Earth's environment but human health as well.

NO_x, SO_x, and CO. When coal, oil, wood, and natural gas are burned, they emit waste products into the air. Coal in particular is a source of several pollutants, including nitrogen oxides (NO_x), sulfur dioxide (SO_2), carbon monoxide (CO), and particulate matter, tiny carbon particles. Each of these substances can cause illness, particularly among people with respiratory problems. When these substances react with other compounds in the atmosphere, more widespread and serious problems arise.

Acid Deposition. When sulfur dioxide and nitrogen oxides are released into the air, they are transformed chemically into acids, specifically sulfuric acid (H_2SO_4) and nitric acid (HNO_3). These compounds eventually fall to Earth in a process called

Industrial plants often have to dispose of large amounts of excess, or waste, heat. This row of giant cooling towers evaporates water, releasing heat into the atmosphere along with a haze of water vapor.

acid deposition. The compounds sometimes fall in dry form. More commonly, however, they combine with water vapor in the air and fall as acid precipitation, which may take the form of acid snow, acid fog, acid hail, or the infamous acid rain. Acid precipitation may fall many kilometers from its original pollution source.

Evidence of the widespread nature of the acid-rain problem first appeared in Scandinavia in the early 1950s, when fishers found lakes with no fish. Similar findings were soon made in the Adirondack Mountains of upstate New York and in eastern Canada. The water in the lakes had become so acidic that aquatic life could not survive. As is usually the case with nature's food webs, the effects are not limited to the lake itself. When fish are gone, waterfowl stop coming, as do other birds and mammals that feed on the fish. The ecology of the entire

ENVIROBIT

The pH level of fog in the Los Angeles, California, area has been measured as low as 2—an acidity comparable to lemon juice.

area is altered, as some of these creatures might have been responsible for keeping the local insect population under control. The long-term effects of dead lakes are still unknown.

The damage from acid precipitation is not limited to aquatic food webs. Many scientists now believe that acid rain has caused forests in parts of Europe and North America to grow more slowly or, in some cases, fail to grow at all. The acid may make plants more vulnerable to disease and insects, and studies have shown that acid causes nutrients to leach from the soil. Recently, scientists have found that acid fog seems most responsible for alpine tree deaths. Since many of the trees are at high elevations, they are often surrounded by fog. In areas affected by sulfuric-acid deposition, the fog can take on acid particles and concentrate them into an acid mist. This mist surrounds the tops of the trees and weakens the needles. The trees consequently lose their tolerance for the cold and die during the harsh winter months. In addition, marble statues and limestone monuments in northeastern U.S. cities and as far away as Greece have crumbled, as the acid attacks calcium carbonate in the stone.

Acid rain has not been shown to have any direct impact on human health. Indirectly, the effects are numerous. When coal is combusted, it releases mercury (Hg) as well as other waste products into the air. When mercury eventually is deposited on a lake, acids in the lake convert it into a toxic form. Animals living in the water bioaccumulate the mercury, which can have serious health ramifications when the fish or other aquatic life are eaten by humans. Acidic water can also corrode lead pipes. Lead then enters drinking-water supplies and can

potentially damage human physiology, especially in children.

Reduction of Acid Deposition. Acid rain can be reduced if power plants switch from sulfur-rich coal to low-sulfur coal and oil. Cleaner coal can be created through several methods, one of which is simply cleaning it before combustion with chemicals and water to remove the sulfur. Another method is the use of scrubbers, devices in which the exhaust from power plants is passed through a spray of lime and water. These can be fitted below the tops of smokestacks to catch SO_2 and NO_x emissions. The emissions are later disposed of in sludge form. Finally, emissions can be reduced through energy conservation—the lower the demand for energy, the lower the amount of fuel needed to generate it.

Awareness of the acid-precipitation problem and its major causes has led to laws limiting emissions of sulfur dioxide. Following passage in the United States of the Clean Air Act amendments of 1970, some power plants installed taller smokestacks. While these improved the air quality locally, winds merely carried pollutants farther away. Countries such as Japan and France are relying more on nuclear power to deal with the problem. Other countries encourage the use of scrubbers which, like other sulfur-control devices, are expensive. The technology to burn coal more cleanly exists. While most industrialized countries agree that protecting the environment is worth the cost, they are making slow progress in controlling sulfur emissions.

Greenhouse Gases and Global Warming. In the meantime, another threat to the environment, also linked to power-plant emissions, has appeared. Over the past century, scientists have calculated that levels of carbon dioxide (CO_2) in Earth's atmosphere have been steadily increasing. This phenomenon is believed to be associated with the burning of fossil fuels and the clearing of forests. The carbon produced by fossil-fuel combustion combines with oxygen molecules in the air to create carbon dioxide. Because huge tracts of South American rain forest have been cleared, fewer plants are available to consume carbon dioxide through photosynthesis.

This increases the potential for a hotter greenhouse effect. Like the glass of a greenhouse, carbon dioxide and several other gases can trap the Sun's heat in the Earth's atmosphere, leading to what some scientists call global warming. An average global temperature increase of only a few degrees could have serious effects. If the buildup of carbon dioxide is not halted, some scientists envision major climatic changes, possibly even melting the polar ice caps. Most scientists agree that production and use of fossil fuels is the major human-made contributor to the greenhouse effect.

Curbing the amount of greenhouse gases in the atmosphere is a global concern and a global challenge. Currently, the best solutions involve reducing the use of fossil fuels and increasing the efficiency of power plants so that less waste is released. In fact, these practices, along with expanded use of alternative energy sources, offer the most promise for reducing all forms of air pollution.

LAND POLLUTION

Energy consumption has caused pollution of Earth's land as well—from the disturbance of land by mining to the alteration of an area where a power plant is built to the dumping of waste from its operation. When energy is used, most habitats are affected. Strip mining for coal and mineral resources involves great excavations of earth and often results in permanent scarring or alteration of the land. The extraction of oil and natural gas also has serious impacts on the land, as leaks from the process can seep into the surrounding soil. When power plants are built, large areas of land are affected. Hydroelectric plants in particular can lead to the inundation of thousands of hectares (acres) of land.

The production of electricity creates many tons of waste products that must be disposed of in some manner. Radioactive wastes from nuclear plants present the most serious hazard. Some of these wastes must be kept secure for thousands of years because

As people move their homes into forested areas, as with this modernistic "saucer" house in Colorado, any condition that might damage the forest, such as acid precipitation, comes literally "close to home."

the radioactivity continues to pose health threats for that long. But coal-powered plants also produce great quantities of ash and slag. In China, for example, where coal is the leading fuel, experts estimate that more than 91 million metric tons (100 million tons) of ash and slag are produced each year.

WATER POLLUTION

Erosion. Erosion from surface-mining operations poses a threat to surrounding bodies of water. Laws in many countries require that strip-mined sites be restored as closely as possible to their original state. This can take years, however, and in the meantime, areas to be mined are exposed to the forces of erosion. Sediment is carried by wind and rain down to creeks, rivers, and lakes in the area. These waters and the aquatic life within them can be choked with sediment if adequate control measures are not taken. In addition, these sediments frequently contain poisonous chemicals and acids that can endanger aquatic ecosystems. Even underground mining operations can be hazardous to water in the area. Toxic chemicals and acids drain from these mines into surrounding creeks and other bodies of water.

Leaks. Another threat to water supplies is leaking underground storage tanks. Virtually every gas station stores its gasoline in large underground tanks, which over a period of years can develop leaks. When leaks go undetected, gasoline can seep down through the soil and end up in groundwater, a major source of drinking water in many regions.

Oil Spills. One of the more dramatic threats to Earth's water comes from oil spills. Fragile coastal areas are particularly vulnerable when huge oil tankers run aground. Oil-soaked beaches and wildlife are the most visible signs of these environmental disasters. Less dramatic but also serious are threats to streams and groundwater supplies caused by leaking oil and natural gas. An overturned truck on a highway can leak diesel fuel into a fragile ecosystem. Surprisingly large amounts of oil get into the ocean from the simple oil changes that cars get every few thousand kilometers (miles) — if the old oil is not disposed of properly.

Hydroelectric Plants. Hydroelectric plants can alter aquatic ecosystems and reduce water quality. A free-flowing stream or river contained behind a huge dam allows for silt to build up in the reservoir instead of flowing downstream. The still water of a reservoir frequently becomes warm and stagnant and is subject to greater evaporation, which can alter the mineral content of the water. Aquatic plant and animal life can be adversely affected.

OTHER FORMS OF POLLUTION

While air, land, and water pollution are among the most serious threats to the environment and human health, the use of energy creates other forms of pollution as well. Among these are heat pollution, light pollution, noise pollution, and sight pollution. Although such forms of pollution may not threaten lives, they can be aesthetic menaces.

Heat. Scientists have observed that average temperatures in a city can be more than 3°C (5.4°F) higher than surrounding suburban areas. Infrared cameras on satellites can easily detect these urban heat islands. A number of factors contribute to the higher temperatures. People, buildings, concrete, industries, pavement, and vehicles all generate and/or absorb heat. By blocking winds, buildings help stagnate the air. Cities also leave less room for trees which, through evapotranspiration during photosynthesis, release cooling water from their leaves into the air. Urban heat islands demand more resources since more energy is required to keep them cool. They also can adversely affect human health.

Light. Since its earliest development, electricity has been widely used to light cities. Electric lights have made cities and highways safer while also making it possible for people to function usefully after dark. The lighting needs of different areas vary greatly. In some large cities, half the light radiated is wasted on the empty sky. In some areas, laws have been passed limiting the height and/or wattage of light sources. If light from one property, for example, shines too brightly or creates glare on another property, this can be considered "light trespass," and the offending light source may have to be changed.

Long after the ore runs out, abandoned mines can remain as eyesores, poor growth areas for plants, and dangerous traps for children or amateur explorers. This abandoned mine is in Queensland, Australia.

Light pollution also creates problems for astronomers. For telescopes to function properly, they are used during the evening to provide the darkest backdrop possible to detect faraway heavenly bodies. In southern California, there are so many lights on in the evening that two of the world's largest telescopes are experiencing difficulties detecting far-off stars and planets.

Noise. Energy production and consumption cause wide-ranging noise pollution. Silence is a rare commodity in a busy, industrial world. Regulations exist in many areas limiting noise to levels that are thought not to be damaging to human hearing. Nonetheless, energy production, industrial processes, transportation networks, and even household appliances create noise that is often disturbing. The noises are generated by moving parts of machines,

such as motors or grinders. The rubbing, or friction, of these parts sends out noises in varying volumes. Noise from automobiles is created by the combustion of fuel and oxygen in the engine as well as by the tires rotating over the road. Some neighborhoods and cities have erected soundwalls to help protect residents from the harsh noise of nearby highways.

Sight. Energy use can obstruct our vision in several significant ways. Pollutants from automobiles and from stationary plants that burn fossil fuels contribute to haze and smog, which can seriously reduce visibility. Not only is haze a hazard to vehicular and air traffic, it can also inhibit nature's beauty. At the Grand Canyon in Arizona, for example, haze from West Coast smog and urban power plants frequently obscures the vista.

AUTOMOBILE EMISSIONS

Almost all modern automobiles have gasoline-powered internal-combustion engines. Among the waste products generated by automobile engines are hydrocarbons (HC), nitrogen oxides, and carbon monoxide. It is estimated that in the United States automobile emissions make up about half of all air pollution.

The seriousness of the pollution created by automobiles was first noticed in the Los Angeles area before 1950. Although it had very little industry, Los Angeles seemed to have an unusually large amount of air pollution. Even then, many sunny California days were marred by a brownish haze that irritated residents' eyes and throats. Scientists soon discovered that a combination of factors were involved in the strange phenomena. The geography of the region—Los Angeles is surrounded by mountains on three sides—means that pollutants can easily be trapped there. First and foremost, however, is the heavy reliance on automobiles in the area. Sunlight interacts with the nitrogen oxides and hydrocarbons from car exhausts, creating ozone (O_3). Unlike natural ozone in the upper atmosphere, which serves to protect Earth from harmful ultraviolet radiation, ground-level ozone is a dangerous pollutant. It threatens human health and can damage plants and animals as well as construction materials. Ozone is particularly dangerous for the millions of people who suffer from respiratory diseases, such as asthma and emphysema. Ozone is also a component of another environmental problem—smog. In addition to ozone, smog contains a number of other hazardous chemicals, including a particularly damaging compound known as peroxyacetyl nitrate (PAN), which is the main eye and nose irritant in smog. Smog is formed when strong sunlight acts on a mixture of nitrogen oxides and volatile organic compounds (VOCs).

The auto-pollution problem, although first noticed in Los Angeles, is found around the world. Mexico City regularly exceeds ozone levels set by the World Health Organization (WHO). As with the situation in Los Angeles, geography also plays a part in Mexico City's problem, as do the many factories found throughout the city. Yet far more damaging are the city's 3 million vehicles, which may contribute more than 80% of the pollutants. Smog is sometimes trapped over the city for weeks at a time. Scientists believe that auto emissions also play a role in the urban heat-island phenomenon. Many urban areas in lesser-developed countries (LDCs) face problems with auto emissions. Few, if any, laws exist to control auto emissions in LDCs.

Due in large part to the Clean Air Act of 1970 and its subsequent amendments, pollution control has been forced upon the U.S. auto industry. The act established emission standards that were to be phased in over a period of years. Engine modifications and increased use of lead-free gasoline helped considerably in meeting the standards. But it was the

A soundwall helps protect a neighborhood from a highway's rush-hour noise but also disrupts local habitats and blocks the view. Some countries, such as the Netherlands, have raised up wooded hills or "berms" along highways, but this requires that the land be set aside.

CASE STUDY: THE IMPACT OF AN ELECTRICAL PLANT ON THE ENVIRONMENT

Electric power has transformed modern life. The generation, transmission, and use of electricity have a number of effects on the environment. Large power plants are the most efficient producers of electricity, and most power plants are located near their major users. The plants themselves are huge, and often include large buildings, smokestacks, and transportation facilities. They can usually be seen and often heard over a great distance, contributing both sight and noise pollution to the surrounding area. Hydroelectric plants rely on dams and reservoirs to store the water that powers them. Huge areas of land can be inundated when a hydroelectric plant is built.

serious health hazards for people in the area as well as for the environment.

Electric power plants, by the nature of their operation, produce a great deal of waste heat. Steam is used in power plants

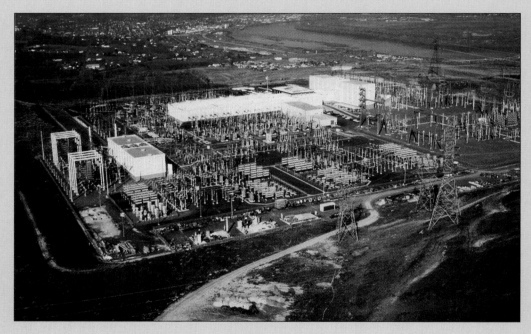

Electric power plants, transformers, and power lines can occupy fairly large tracts of land, often in otherwise natural sites separated from cities.

Most electric plants are powered by fossil fuels, nuclear power, or hydroelectric generators. In the United States, coal is by far the most widely used fuel. Coal burning is the major contributor of sulfur dioxide to the atmosphere. It is also responsible for a variety of other pollutants, many of which affect the area closest to the plant most severely. Properly functioning nuclear plants have very few emissions, but inadvertent leaks of radioactivity, even in small amounts, can pose

to drive turbines, which in turn create electricity. After leaving the turbine, steam must be condensed back into water before it can be reused in the boiler. Some plants simply exhaust the heat from cooling towers into the atmosphere. Many more rely on water to take the waste heat away. The heated water is then discharged into a nearby river or lake. This process can seriously affect aquatic ecosystems, perhaps causing different plants to grow or encouraging fish to spawn at the wrong time of year. Electric power plants generate other waste products as well. Whether it is the radioactive wastes from a nuclear plant or tons of ash and waste from a coal-burning plant, the waste products must be disposed of, ideally with as little damage to the environment as possible.

Once the electricity is generated, it must be transmitted to its final users. This is usually accomplished through overhead wires. In some areas, particularly those close to power plants, the huge network of overhead transmission lines can be an eyesore. Even in rural areas, long stretches of roadways are frequently flanked by power lines. Some urban areas are too crowded for overhead wires, requiring the use of underground cables to transmit electricity. This option is considered too expensive to use on a wide scale.

Sight pollution created by transmission lines is one of the prices paid for convenient access to electric power. Another concern regarding electric lines is their potential to harm human health. When electricity is moved over electric lines or used by appliances, a magnetic field is created. Although scientists have not been able to determine the method, some studies have shown a correlation between exposure to magnetic fields and the incidence of childhood leukemia. Foundations and utility companies are working together to reduce magnetic fields surrounding the lines and appliances without reducing the distribution of electricity.

In the United States, electricity is distributed to customers by more than 4.8 million kilometers (2.9 million miles) of transmission and distribution lines, and over 300,000 kilometers (186,410 miles) of underground cables.

widespread use of a device called the catalytic converter that brought about substantial reductions in the emission of hydrocarbons and nitrogen oxides. The catalytic converter is attached to an automobile's exhaust pipe. Exhaust gases and outside air pass through metallic beads in the device. These beads help convert the hydrocarbons and carbon monoxide to carbon dioxide and water. Despite the progress that has been made, automobile exhausts are still very dirty.

The U.S. government has also established air-quality standards which many cities have failed to meet. Weather forecasters in many localities include data on levels of ozone and other pollutants present in the air. The air around a large number of major U.S. cities is still dubbed "unhealthful" on many days of the year. In 1990, for example, the air in Los Angeles was categorized as unhealthful 163 days. According to some estimates, the average ozone concentrations in industrialized cities of North America and Europe are up to three times higher than the level at which damage to vegetation begins. The problem can extend to rural areas as well. Some studies attribute crop losses of more than $5 billion in the United States to ozone damage.

In cities around the world, the situation is even worse. Leaded gasoline is still used in cities such as New Delhi, India; Kuala Lumpur, Malaysia; and Bangkok, Thailand. Many of the cars in these countries are old, and catalytic converters are not attached to the exhaust pipes. Even in more developed countries, older, poorly maintained cars may contribute half of all pollutants to the air. The U.S. Environmental Protection Agency (EPA) requires emissions testing in areas where air quality does not meet federal standards. But even if emissions from individual automobiles do meet standards, this improvement may be largely offset by the increasing number of vehicles on the road.

Proposed Solutions. Several solutions have been suggested for addressing the auto-emissions problem. Cleaner-burning gasoline is now being sold in some U.S. cities. In addition, gas stations may be required to install vapor collection systems on gas

The exhaust gases from an automobile may be so full of unburned and partly burned particles that a dirty cloud is visible. Yet some of the deadliest gases in the exhaust are invisible, such as carbon monoxide.

ENVIROBIT

There are about eight times more cars in the world today than there were in 1950.

pumps, since a surprising amount of harmful vapors can escape during a single fill-up. Another initiative involves the manufacture of vehicles that use alternate fuels. California is leading the way in this

Vancouver, British Columbia, is on Canada's wind-blown west coast, at the foot of wild mountains; yet even here industrial and automotive emissions sometimes build into a citywide haze.

endeavor. The state is requiring that all automobile makers who sell more than 3,000 vehicles in California manufacture certain percentages of zero-emission vehicles (ZEVs). Under the plan, 2% of all new cars must be ZEVs by 1998. By 2001, 5% must be ZEVs, and by 2003, 10% must be ZEVs. California's mandate has created a new market for automakers. It is hoped that the industry will embrace the idea and try to sell ZEVs in other states.

ZEVs may pave the way for increased production of electric automobiles. Because electric power is far more efficient than gasoline, these vehicles conserve fuel and energy. Electric cars have no emissions, require little maintenance, and in a traffic jam can be turned off like a television set. These cars are still expensive, however, and the production, refueling, and disposal of batteries would present a different set of environmental concerns. In the meantime, and

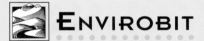

ENVIROBIT

Over the course of its lifetime, a new car with pollution controls will spew out some 136 kilograms (300 pounds) of smog-forming compounds, and 31 metric tons (34 tons) of carbon monoxide.

perhaps in the long run, greater reliance on public transportation may be a practical solution. Not only will more people be transported with fewer pollutants, but less fuel will be consumed as well.

INDUSTRIAL POLLUTION

While automobile emissions and the burning of fossil fuels contribute the majority of pollution to the atmosphere, industrial facilities also pollute the environment with sulfur dioxide, carbon monoxide, particulate matter, and a variety of volatile organic compounds (VOCs). For example, when organic solvents used in paints and cleaning fluids evaporate, hydrocarbons are emitted into the atmosphere. The metal smelting industry, which makes metals from ore, emits large quantities of sulfur, increasing sulfur dioxide levels in some areas. Refuse incineration can add significantly to the amount of particulate matter in the air.

In addition, as heavy users of electricity, industries indirectly contribute to the pollution created by power plants. Industries waste a great deal of energy, which means that electric power plants have to produce more electricity. Factory pumps and motors frequently operate at high speeds and, therefore, require a great deal of energy. Some experts estimate that industry could reduce its electricity consumption by 50% by improving maintenance procedures and using variable-speed motors.

Industry is also responsible for contributing a wide variety of toxic materials to the air, land, and water. According to a 1989 U.S. government survey, 22,560 industrial facilities released 2.58 billion kilograms (5.7 billion pounds) of toxic chemicals into the environment. Fortunately, disasters like the one that occurred on December 4, 1984, at a Union Carbide plant in Bhopal, India, do not happen often. In that incident, more than 3,800 people were killed and over 200,000 more injured when a cloud of methyl isocyanate gas, a toxic gas used to make pesticides, leaked from the chemical plant. The gas escaped from its storage tank after a hose was accidentally attached to a pressure-gauge opening, which injected 454 to 908 liters (120 to 240 gal-

Electric vehicles like this experimental van are already operational, but persuading large numbers of people to buy them may depend on having networks of fast-operating recharging stations.

ENVIROBIT

According to the U.S. Environmental Protection Agency (EPA), lead concentrations in the atmosphere dropped by 89% between 1982 and 1991, mainly because leaded gasoline is no longer commonly used.

lons) of water into the tank. The water and other liquids combined to create chloroform, which, under the pressure of the tank, exploded. Systems that should have prevented the accident, such as scrubbers and refrigerators, were not in service because of neglect. The accident brought worldwide attention to the problem of air pollution. Lesser-developed nations became particularly concerned, as they host the facilities of many large, multinational corporations. Today, the volume of hazardous materials that industries routinely emit into our air, either through industrial processes or accidents, remains quite high.

Many companies use chemicals to make a variety of products, from plastics to pesticides, foods to fibers. Automobile manufacturers, meat processors, paper mills, and weapons manufacturers, to name just a few, use and dispose of a wide variety of chemical compounds. Metal processing companies, for example, produce wastes that contain heavy metals, such as lead (Pb), mercury (Hg), arsenic (As), and cadmium (Cd). Exposure to even small doses of these heavy metals can cause serious physiological and neurological damage. A group of chemicals called xylenes are used in manufacturing drugs, dyes, and insecticides. Chemicals such as methanol (H_3OH) are used as solvents and cleaning materials in many industries. Ammonia (NH_3), a colorless gas, is used to make fertilizers, plastics, dyes, and textiles. A pleasant-smelling liquid called methylene chloride (CH_2Cl), which is used in food, plastics and furniture processing, and paint removers, irritates the skin, eyes, nose, and throat and can cause pulmonary edema or even death. These are just a few of the chemicals used in industry. Once

used, chemical waste products must be disposed of. Many chemical wastes contain extremely hazardous substances that can be explosive, flammable, corrosive, or poisonous.

Disposal of Wastes.   Traditionally, industries have disposed of their hazardous wastes by either emitting them into the air or flushing them out with water into nearby rivers and lakes. Such practices continue in many parts of the world. In the United States and several other Western nations, legislation has restricted discharge of waste into the air and water. The Clean Air Act of 1970 and the Clean Water Act of 1970 have brought about some dramatic improvements. Levels of dichloro-diphenyl-trichloro-ethane (DDT) and polychlorinated biphenyls (PCBs) in the Great Lakes, for example, have dropped sub-

After poisonous fumes spread from a Union Carbide pesticide plant in Bhopal, India, the world saw many news photos like this one of a mother and child awaiting medical treatment. Nearly 4,000 people died.

ENVIROBIT

Nearly 91 million kilograms (200 million pounds) of ammonia were released into the air over the United States in 1991.

stantially since the mid-1970s. Subsequent amendments to these acts have placed further limits on air and water discharges.

Although industries have reduced their polluting activities as far as the air and water are concerned, many have turned to disposal on land. One of the most commonly used methods of land disposal involves drilling deep wells into porous material below the groundwater level. Theoretically, the hazardous materials pumped into the wells will slowly soak down into the ground but should not affect the groundwater above. Some hazardous wastes are deposited along with large quantities of water in pits or ponds sealed with a plastic liner. As the water evaporates, the wastes settle to the bottom of the pit. Still another method of disposing of

hazardous waste is by putting it into drums that are then buried in a specially designed site.

Environmental Impact. These disposal methods can pose serious risks to the surrounding land and particularly to the groundwater supply. Should the wastes from any of these storage facilities leak into the groundwater, the situation would be nearly impossible to correct. Groundwater disperses through the soil over a large area, making monitoring and cleanup very difficult. In 1980, the United States created a special program to deal with the most hazardous waste sites in the country. Commonly known as Superfund, the program levied a special tax on chemical companies, the proceeds of which are used to clean up the most hazardous sites. While this has helped in a limited number of cases, the situation is often so dire that the area is simply closed off and secured.

In reaction to stricter laws in the United States and other developed countries, many industries have moved some of their more hazardous operations overseas. Lesser-developed countries frequently welcome these operations since they employ local people and contribute much needed money to the

The Department of Energy's Waste Isolation Pilot Plant in New Mexico is an experimental underground facility to demonstrate ways to store powerful transuranic radioactive wastes. It is drilled into a salt rock formation. This formation is being tested to find out if it can safely keep the waste out of contact with the environment.

country's treasury. Environmental protection, therefore, is not always their top priority.

Monitoring and Control. As a first step, better controls over the production and disposal of solid wastes are needed. In 1976, the Congress passed the Resource Conservation and Recovery Act (RCRA). This act, and its later amendments, requires strict recordkeeping on hazardous wastes. The production, transfer, and disposal of such wastes must be recorded, and all facilities that handle hazardous wastes are required to have permits and meet strict standards. The monitoring of hazardous materials from the time they are created to the time they are disposed of is referred to as the cradle-to-grave practice. This covers the period of manufacturing, treatment, transportation, storage, and disposal of waste materials. The RCRA also established criteria to regulate the operation of disposal sites. The EPA began to manage disposal sites and could halt operations if the site was deemed unsafe. Enforcement of these regulations is difficult, however, and smaller producers of toxic wastes and ordinary municipal solid waste that may have traces of hazardous waste mixed in are exempt from the restrictions.

Another approach to dealing with industrial pollution is for producers to make a more concerted effort to create fewer hazardous wastes in the first place. New production methods could result in fewer toxic by-products or in more easily processed and recycled materials. Recycling of materials can result in substantial energy savings as well. In some cases, only half as much energy is used to make products such as paper and glass from recycled materials than from raw materials.

POLLUTION FROM HOME CONSUMPTION

Most individuals do not consider that their daily activities contribute to environmental-pollution problems. In fact, the amount of pollution generated by people in their homes is small. But there are a surprising number of ways in which we do contribute to the problem, and almost as many ways in which we can help solve it.

Humans are users of energy 24 hours a day. Our homes are comfortably heated and cooled by electricity, oil, or natural gas. As soon as we wake up in the morning we turn on lights and use electric appliances. The power plant that supplies the electricity may well be burning coal or oil, spewing a variety of pollutants into the atmosphere. We drive to work or school in a car or bus that is probably exhausting hydrocarbons and carbon monoxide. When we practice conservation, we not only save resources, we also protect the environment.

Many more individual activities add to pollution problems. People who smoke can create a hazardous environment inside their own homes. Cigarette smoke contains carbon monoxide, aldehydes, and benzene. Gas stoves and furnaces are also sources of carbon monoxide. Smoke from wood-burning stoves or even fires in a fireplace contribute a surprising amount of particulate matter to the air. The once common practice of backyard leaf burning has been banned in many communities because the resulting smoke carries harmful particulates.

Homeowners regularly handle a number of toxic materials. The warning labels on paints, insecticides, drain cleaners, and other cleaning products indicate the kind of poisonous substances these products contain. Although people often handle such substances carefully while using them, when it comes time to dispose of the materials, they are often poured into the sink or thrown out with the rest of the trash. Ultimately, these products end up in a sewage-treatment plant, an incinerator, or a landfill, where they can pollute the air, land, and water. Similarly, when changing the oil in their cars, people sometimes dispose of the used oil by dumping it down the drain or, even worse, pouring it into a storm drain. Oil poured down a storm drain ends up directly in a stream or river, with no treatment whatsoever.

Many communities are attempting to work with homeowners by having special trash collections for hazardous household materials or by encouraging service stations to accept discarded oil for recycling. These options are not always available, however, and when they are, they are not always well publicized.

Gardeners attempting to beautify their surroundings often do so at great cost to the environment. They rely on fertilizers, weedkillers, pesticides, and other hazardous chemicals to grow greener lawns, more beautiful flowers, and tastier fruits and vegetables. Lawn-improvement companies promise spectacular results, but the cost in dollars and in environmental damage can be high. Chemicals applied in sprays can end up in the air as well as on the lawn. Those applied as powders or granules can wash down into the soil, benefiting the lawn but potentially damaging groundwater. In addition, numerous insects, birds, and other wildlife may be harmed as these substances work their way up the food chain. Sprinklers or rain may allow the chemicals to run off into the road, down a storm drain, and into a nearby stream.

Gasoline-powered gardening equipment, such as power lawn mowers, leaf blowers, shredders, and string trimmers, can contribute to noise pollution in a neighborhood. Like gasoline-powered automobiles, they also contribute to air pollution. Using a leaf blower for one hour creates as much air pollution as driving a car more than 160 kilometers (100 miles). For this reason, these tools have been banned in Los Angeles.

Just as individuals can contribute to pollution problems, they can also work to solve them. Leaves can be raked and recycled through composting, rather than packed in plastic bags and taken to a landfill. Energy-intensive products, or products that used a lot of energy when manufactured, can be recycled as well, including aluminum cans, glass and plastic bottles, and newspapers. Many communities have organized recycling programs that depend on resident participation. When plastic containers are reused, a factory will produce fewer toxic chemicals since they will have to produce fewer containers. Frequently, less energy is required to produce goods from recycled materials than from raw materials. For example, the energy expended by a forest-product company to harvest trees and get them to a paper mill can be substantially reduced by recycling paper products. In the process, trees are saved as well.

We can conserve resources for future generations by reducing energy use today. When people leave their cars at home and walk or ride a bike instead, less gasoline is used and fewer auto emissions are sent into the air. By turning off lights in a room that is not being used or using a knife to chop vegetables rather than a food processor, less electricity is consumed. In turn, the electric utility burns a little less coal, which results in decreased air pollution. When these savings are multiplied by millions of people, a little bit of conservation can make a big difference.

Sources

American Chemical Society. *ChemCom: Chemistry in the Community*. Dubuque, IA: Kendall/Hunt, 1988.

Corson, Walter, ed. *The Global Ecology Handbook*. Boston: Beacon Press, 1990.

Cozic, Charles P., ed. *Pollution. Current Controversies Series*. San Diego, CA: Greenhaven Press, 1994.

Golob, Richard, and Eric Brus. *The Almanac of Renewable Energy*. New York: Henry Holt, World Information Systems, 1993.

Nebel, Bernard J. *Environmental Science: The Way the World Works*. 2nd ed. Englewood Cliffs, NJ: Prentice-Hall, 1987.

World Energy Council. *Energy for Tomorrow's World*. New York: St. Martin's Press, 1993.

World Resources Institute. *The 1994 Information Please Environmental Almanac*. Boston: Houghton Mifflin, 1994.

Alternative Energy and Conservation

Humans have long known of the need to find replacements for the dwindling supplies of fossil fuels. While we have been spurred at times by energy crises, our dedication to the task of finding alternative energy sources has wavered. Progress has been made in many areas, but no permanent solution to the energy problem has been found. The technology to exploit alternative energy sources is still being developed. In the meantime, environmental pollution caused by fossil fuels has created a new sense of urgency. As the search continues for the energy source of the future, the need to conserve our resources and to use them more efficiently becomes even more critical.

THE HISTORY OF ALTERNATIVE FUELS

Fossil fuels will not last forever. The processes that formed them eons ago below the Earth's surface cannot create them now. Although fossil fuels are nonrenewable resources, as long as we are able to access them for our immediate needs, it is difficult to focus on the future. Historically, only crises have jarred our sense of security.

Political Links. In 1973, political turmoil in the Middle East led to an interruption in the flow

ENVIROBIT

According to the U.S. Environmental Protection Agency, the energy to run buildings in the United States costs about $70 billion a year.

of oil to many industrialized countries. Europeans, Americans, and Japanese in particular realized how dependent they had become on foreign oil. Conservation became the watchword of the time. Governments in most developed countries committed themselves to "energy independence," a phrase that meant different things in different countries. France and Japan, for instance, made a renewed commitment to nuclear power. In most countries, however, at least some commitment was made to exploring alternative fuels.

Governments play an important role in the development of alternative energy sources. Many of the technologies required to make use of renewable energy sources are expensive, especially in the early stages of development. New technologies have to be tested,

During 1973, when headlines warned of oil shortages, fearful U.S. motorists took every opportunity to fill up. Here a Manhattan gas station opened on a Sunday (despite President Nixon's urging stations to stay closed). When motorists on the Queensboro Bridge above the station saw the open pumps, large numbers of them detoured down from the bridge to join the lines for gas.

and demonstration projects sometimes fail. Few individuals or companies are willing to take such financial risks. In the late 1970s and early 1980s, the U.S. government offered numerous incentives to encourage the development of alternative resources. For example, tax credits were offered to developers of wind farms and to homeowners who installed solar heating units in their homes. The 1978 Public Utilities Regulatory Policy Act required that utilities purchase electricity from independent producers. Ethanol-blended gasolines were exempt from federal taxes. Government funding was offered for research and development of new energy resources. During this period of great enthusiasm, more than 1 million residential solar water-heating systems were installed. Nearly 400 megawatts of electricity were produced from various solar projects. In 1981, the Department of Energy envisioned 20% of U.S. energy consumption coming from renewable resources by the year 2000.

But then the crisis situation subsided. Conservation measures paid off, oil prices dropped, and the immediate future did not look quite so bleak. Government deficits became more of a concern. By the end of 1985, most government tax incentives for the development of alternative resources had expired. In just four years, from 1981 to 1985, government spending on renewable energy was cut by more than $500 million. Funding has increased only slightly from its low point in 1990.

In 1980, U.S. government appropriations for renewable energy amounted to more than $800 million. In 1993, the amount appropriated was less than $250 million.

While concern about future energy resources is not as urgent as it was in the late 1970s and early 1980s, new concerns have been raised about the future of Earth's environment. The use of fossil fuels has contributed substantially to global pollu-

tion problems. Renewable energy sources have been targeted to relieve some of the worry.

BIOMASS

Biomass is energy derived from living things. As plants convert sunlight, water, and carbon dioxide (CO_2) into carbohydrates and oxygen in photosynthesis, they store the Sun's energy in their tissues. By burning this plant material, chemical energy can be converted into heat or other forms of energy. Over the course of human history, biomass in the form of fuelwood provided the most energy. Even today in less-developed regions of the world, such as Asia and Africa, biomass frequently supplies anywhere from 50% to 90% of all the energy used.

As industrialized nations encountered one fuel crisis after another since the 1960s, many people began to look again at the possibility of using biomass energy. Trees can be grown, harvested, and used locally, eliminating transportation costs that can be prohibitively high in lesser-developed countries (LDCs). With proper management, biomass can be a renewable energy source.

More than 95% of Nepal's total energy comes from biomass. In industrialized countries, biomass provides an average of less than 3%.

Environmental Impact. Several problems are associated with biomass use. First, because biomass has a low energy density, a large amount must be consumed to produce a usable amount of energy. This has led to serious overharvesting in many parts of the world. In Africa, for example, large expanses of land have been picked bare, leading to soil degradation and erosion. This occurs when deforested areas begin to respond to the lack of vegetation. When plants or trees are cut down more sunlight hits the ground. In some soils, this can dry out the land, making it infertile. And because plant roots hold the soil together, the removal or death of the roots can cause precious topsoil to dry out, loosen, and be blown away by winds or rain. Also, with the reduction of leaf litter—leaves, branches, and seeds that fall off trees—comes a reduction in natural inputs of soil fertilizing material. The loss of those inputs can also cause reduced fertility. Many experts believe that recent famines in Africa can be attributed to soil degradation caused by overharvesting of plant material for fuel. Second, burning of biomass can contribute to air-pollution problems, although not nearly to the extent that fossil fuels do.

Conversion of Biomass. Biomass is generally burned as a solid fuel but can be converted into liquid and gaseous fuels as well. While fuelwood is the most common form of biomass energy, other plant and animal materials can also be used. Agricultural and forest crops can be grown specifically for energy purposes. In some parts of the world, trees are grown on "energy plantations." Studies are under way to determine which species can grow most quickly and produce the most energy. Some energy crops are sorghum, sugarcane, and corn, as well as more unconventional species such as the Jerusalem artichoke and cassava. Many of these crops are grown for the purpose of converting them to liquid fuels such as ethanol.

Wastes from agriculture and forestry, as well as from food and timber processing, can also be used to produce energy. The production of grains and nuts, for example, results in a large quantity of residue in the form of husks and shells. These can be burned for heating, cooking, or even for producing electricity. The pulp and paper industry has long relied on its voluminous wastes to power much of its operations. Domestic and agricultural wastes, particularly manure, can be converted into a gaseous fuel known as biogas. In rural areas of China and India, this form of biomass energy provides heat, light, and electricity for thousands of households. At the same time, it helps solve the problem of dealing with sewage and other wastes. Some communities in developed nations are taking the idea even further by producing energy from municipal solid wastes and sewage. Some areas are using sludge from sewage treatment plants to fertilize forest and agricultural soils.

SOLAR ENERGY

People have long been aware of the abundance of solar energy. Ancient Greeks built their houses in an architectural style that took advantage of the Sun's warmth. Today, passive solar heating systems use heat flow, evaporation, or other natural processes to collect and transfer the Sun's heat. Even on a cold winter day, the Sun's rays pouring through large windows can warm a room to comfortable temperatures. On hot summer days, overhangs or awnings can keep the same room from getting too hot.

ENVIROBIT

In the United States, enough solar energy is received daily to meet the nation's power needs for 18 months.

Active and Passive Solar Energy. The search continues for other ways to make use of the Sun's energy. Active solar heating systems use a flat-plate collector and a system of pumps and pipes to circulate and store the Sun's heat. Installed most often on the roof of a building, a flat-plate solar collector consists of a black surface covered with glass or plastic, which usually encloses tubes of water. The black surface absorbs the Sun's heat, and the glass or plastic keeps the heat from radiating away. Water in the tubes is heated as it passes through the collector. Pumps and pipes then circulate the heated water throughout the building. Active solar heating systems developed thus far are expensive and often subject to mechanical breakdowns. Passive solar systems are simple. One technique is constructing a home or building with many windows facing the Sun.

Both active and passive solar heating systems require backup systems for prolonged periods of

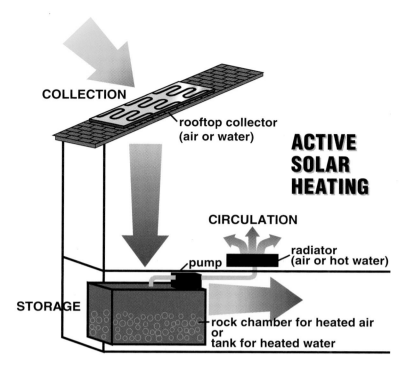

Active solar heating systems use special equipment for the collection, storage, and circulation of heat: rooftop collectors, storage tanks, pumps, and radiators.

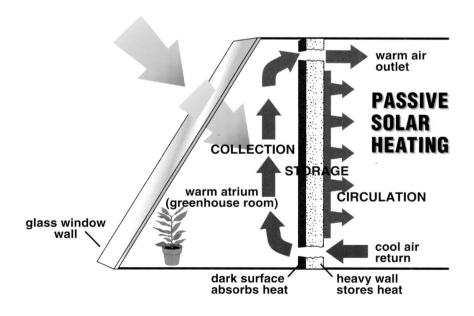

Passive solar systems use the structure of the building itself to collect and store heat, with circulation largely generated naturally, or assisted only by a few fans.

The sloped surfaces of this building expose a large number of solar collectors to sunlight. Note how the gaps in the collecting surface provide airy but shaded balconies for the rooms on each floor. Architecture like this can provide a technological advance and also take care of the comfort of the occupants.

cloudy weather. Whenever they are used to heat air or water, they enable the diminishing supplies of fossil fuels to last a little longer. As part of the endeavor to lessen the dependence on fossil fuels, many efforts are under way to take advantage of solar energy. Most of these focus on ways to convert the Sun's energy to electricity.

ENVIROBIT

In Israel, more than 700,000 households have solar water-heating units. In Japan, more than 4 million solar water heaters are in use.

Photovoltaic Technology. The most promising prospect is the photovoltaic cell. Photovoltaic cells are composed of thin layers of silicon that convert sunlight into electricity. They have no moving parts and rely only on the Sun's light to displace electrons from their orbits to produce electric current. Each cell produces only a small amount of electricity.

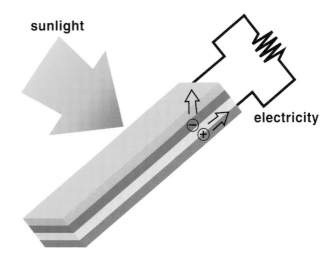

In a photovoltaic cell, sunlight shining in through the transparent top layer strikes a layer of photosensitive crystals, knocking electrons loose to make an electric current.

Solar cells are widely used in calculators and toys. But when large numbers of photovoltaic cells are grouped together, they can produce enough electricity to supply a house, an office building, or even a space station. In fact, solar cells have been used to power space vehicles since the late 1950s. They are also used to bring electricity to remote locations. Photovoltaic cells are still too expensive to use on a large scale. Homeowners, companies, and institutions willing to make the initial investment can install photovoltaic cells on their rooftops, thereby producing a large portion of their own electricity when weather permits. As the cost for solar cells continues to come down, visions of photovoltaic power plants may become a reality.

Solar Cookers. One simple technology that has been used with great success in Africa and Latin America is the solar cooker. People living in rural communities in these areas rely on biomass, low-grade coal, and animal dung for fuels to cook their food and heat their homes. However, cutting down trees to provide enough fuel for rapidly expanding communities is creating huge tracts of deforested areas. The United Nations Food and Agriculture Organization estimates that 84% of Africans will face wood shortages by the end of the 1990s. The burning of the wood for fuel also adds thousands of metric tons of carbon dioxide to the atmosphere every year. The smoke from all of the fuels is responsible for thousands of cases of respiratory, skin, and eye diseases.

Solar cookers provide one method of combating such problems. The cooker looks like a simple wooden box with a glass surface. Pots or containers are placed on a dark, heat-conducting metal plate inside the box. A flip-top lid wrapped in aluminum foil acts as an extra solar panel, channeling more light into the box. In Africa and several areas in Latin America, sunshine is plentiful and strong, making the box a viable cooking tool. In strong sunlight, the ovens can maintain a 177°C (350°F) temperature, which can easily cook foods or boil and purify water. Although the cookers are excellent replacements for polluting fuels, they do have a few drawbacks. They cannot be used at night and

are not very efficient on cloudy days. Cooking times must be altered from the traditional ones. The cooker should be turned every so often to follow the Sun, thereby maximizing the collection of rays.

Solar Collectors. Another method of producing electricity from solar energy involves concentrating the Sun's rays to produce enough heat to boil water. As in a conventional power plant, steam is used to turn turbines and generate electricity. Many elaborate systems are being tested. Trough collector systems made up of U-shaped mirrors have produced temperatures up to 400°C (752°F). "Power towers" employ several hectares (acres) of light-tracking mirrors that focus the Sun's rays on a boiler high atop a tower. Such systems require a considerable amount of space and must be located near the user to avoid losing too much power in transmission. But as supplies of fossil fuels dwindle, populations may well turn to the ultimate source of energy—the Sun.

WIND AND TIDAL POWER

Powered by solar heating of the atmosphere, wind energy is one of humankind's oldest energy sources. The picturesque windmills that helped expand the land area of the Netherlands and provide electricity to farms on the U.S. Great Plains have been replaced by new, aerodynamically designed wind turbines. Huge machines capable of generating 10 megawatts or more of energy have been developed. The blades of these turbines are subject to problems related to vibration and stress. Another new approach involves the development of wind farms, where several hundred small turbines are grouped together. The smaller machines tend to be more reliable and are easier to maintain.

Disadvantages. One disadvantage of wind energy is that it is not constant. Although there are few

ENVIROBIT

Wind farms in California produced more than 2.5 billion kilowatt hours of electricity in 1991.

CASE STUDY: SOLAR VEHICLES

In recent years, pollution from automobiles has become a worldwide concern. High schools and colleges have begun to work on technologies to solve the problem by building cars that are powered by the Sun and batteries. Bringing the school teams together to compete in races has created a lot of publicity that has helped entice major car companies to start projects of their own.

Solar cars use an array of solar panels made of photovoltaic cells to capture a small percentage of the Sun's energy and send it to a series of lead-acid batteries for storage. A motor controller translates the energy and runs the motor. Other than this, a solar car runs much like a regular automobile, although its components are specially designed to be lightweight and aerodynamic. They are sometimes taken from race cars.

The University of Pennsylvania in Philadelphia has developed such a solar car, which has been named *Liberty Belle*. Not only has the project taken great strides in environmental terms, it has offered students of all disciplines a unique learning experience. Students from the various schools of the university work together much like a regular corporation. Business students handle most of the fund-raising and publicity, while engineering students are responsible for the design and construction of the car.

Specifically, electrical-engineering students work on projects such as installing energy-efficient brake lights on the tail of the car, allowing for more efficient use of the vehicle's electrical system. Students of materials science put together the car's lightweight and aerodynamic body. The materials used to construct the body are fabrics that harden into strong and lightweight forms when chemicals are added. The *Liberty Belle* uses carbon fiber, Kevlar (the material used in making bulletproof vests), and a material called Nomex honeycomb. A teaching assistant who gained experience with composite fibers while building kayaks for the 1988 U.S. Olympic Team helped the University of Pennsylvania students learn to work with the materials.

Mechanical engineering plays a large part in the project as well. The brakes, steering system, wheels, and suspension are all key elements on the vehicle. The *Liberty Belle* uses floating hydraulic disk brakes made for sprint-car racing. The steering operates just as in a regular car, although the steering wheel is slightly smaller. The wheels, which are built with the same materials used to make the body, use standard bicycle rims and hubs. The tires are mountain bicycle tires, which can be filled to a high pressure, a necessity for handling the weight of the car. Weight is a key element to success in a solar car race. The *Liberty Belle* weighs about 270 kilograms (600 pounds), while a small gasoline-powered hatchback car is about 907 kilograms (2,000 pounds). At top speed, the car can travel at about 129 kilometers (80 miles) per hour.

Computer-science students work with the car's onboard computer, which can monitor up to 16 sensors around the car that measure such variables as temperature, speed, and battery voltage. The system not only displays the information on a screen that the driver can see, but also sends it to a lap-top computer in the chase car, a vehicle that follows the solar car during a race. Using special computer software, team members in the chase car study how the solar car is running and send instructions to the driver over a two-way radio so the driver can keep the car running at its most efficient level.

Business students work with the university's alumni as well as companies around the country to raise money and seek out parts donations. The cost of building the *Liberty Belle*, not including labor hours, totaled about $50,000. Some teams, especially those run by the major auto companies, spend more than $1 million on developing the high technologies used in their cars. The race cars are used as tests for vehicles that might be available in the future. The *Liberty Belle*, which has been featured on television and in the print media, participates in races that span up to 1,770 kilometers (1,100 miles) in total distance.

Until the next race, the students continue to make improvements on the *Liberty Belle*, hoping to contribute to the growing wealth of knowledge and attention being given to zero-emission vehicles.

The University of Pennsylvania's Liberty Belle *is a solar car created by students.*

places where the wind blows continuously, wind energy has been exploited quite successfully in certain areas. From San Francisco to Denmark to Mongolia, people around the world are getting at least some of their electricity from wind power. Mountain passes, coastlines, and other regions that have the highest sustained winds are the most likely sites for wind farms. While the initial costs of setting up wind turbines and generators can be high, the electricity they provide is essentially free once the apparatus is installed. For this reason, wind energy has particular appeal to developing countries. Although vast expanses of turbines can interfere with scenic views and create a substantial amount of noise, wind turbines produce no emissions that blur vistas and harm human health.

The ebb and flow of tides and the crashing of waves on the beach are constant evidence of the power stored in the sea. Human efforts to harness this energy began centuries ago. Tide-powered mills were built along the coasts of Europe as early as the 11th century. Today, efforts continue in Europe and other parts of the world to harness electricity from the ocean. Technology to extract electricity from waves is not highly developed, but tests are under way in almost every major body of water. Tidal power plants are in operation but are costly and operate for only a portion of the day. In addition, these plants can be built on only a limited number of sites. For tidal plants to produce enough electricity to make their construction worthwhile, the tidal range must be at least 5 meters (16 feet) from low to high tide.

The operation of a tidal plant is similar in some respects to that of a hydroelectric plant. A dam creates a basin or reservoir of water that fills up as the tide rises. The water is held there until the falling tide creates what is called a "head" of water pressure. The water is then released into the sea through a turbine until the level of water is about the same in the basin as it is in the sea. Electricity is usually generated just by holding water in the basin and then releasing it as the tide goes out, although it is also possible to hold the rising tide back in the ocean until a sufficient head

develops. A tidal plant on the Rance River in France has been in operation since 1966 and generates more than 500 megawatts of electricity each year.

Environmental Impact. Tidal plants can inflict environmental harm. They can alter tidal ranges and currents as well as water temperature and quality. The construction of facilities can trap sediments and hamper the migration of marine animals. Shipping and even recreational use of the region can be affected. Most experts do not envision tidal power as a major source of energy, although it can make a substantial contribution in a few locations.

HYDROGEN

Hydrogen (H), one of the world's most plentiful elements, offers much promise in meeting future energy needs. It burns cleanly and, when used as a fuel, combines with oxygen to produce water vapor. Hydrogen, however, rarely exists in a pure form. It is almost always already combined with oxygen in the form of water. In order to obtain usable hydrogen, molecules of water must be split—a process that requires energy.

Hydrogen is a versatile element that can be produced from many substances in addition to water. It can be used as a liquid to fuel vehicles or as a gas that can be transported great distances by pipeline to provide heat. Hydrogen is used for industrial processes such as petroleum refining and ammonia (NH_3) and methanol production. Most of the hydrogen currently in use is derived from fossil fuels, particularly natural gas. Obtaining hydrogen with energy from fossil fuels negates most of its value, so researchers are exhaustively searching for economical methods to produce it.

A character in Jules Verne's 1874 book *The Mysterious Island* declared: "I believe that water will one day be employed as a fuel, that hydrogen and oxygen which constitute it, used singularly or together, will furnish an inexhaustible source of heat and light."

A rocket bearing a U.S. space shuttle uses hydrogen fuel to power its lift-off from Earth.

Scientists have been studying the process of photosynthesis to see if this offers possibilities for producing hydrogen. In the initial photosynthetic reactions, light energy separates water molecules into hydrogen and oxygen. The hydrogen atoms then quickly attach to carbon (C) atoms. If researchers can find a way to duplicate the process and halt photosynthesis after the first step, hydrogen might be available in abundance. Research in this area is in a very early stage.

Electrolysis has already been used to produce hydrogen from water. This method involves passing electrical energy through water, which causes water molecules to split into hydrogen and oxygen. Currently, the cost of the electricity used is greater than the value of the hydrogen energy produced. Electrolysis driven by photovoltaic cells has been demonstrated and would be a viable alternative if the cost of the solar cells continues to decline.

Use of Hydrogen. If technology becomes available to produce hydrogen cheaply, ways must also be developed to transport, store, and distribute it safely. Natural-gas pipelines could be modified to transport hydrogen. This would cost much less than transporting electricity over transmission lines. Unlike electricity, hydrogen can be stored in a number of ways. At normal temperatures and pressures, hydrogen is a very low-density gas. Its density can be increased by storing it under high pressure or cooling it until it liquefies. Internal-combustion engines, with a few modifications, can burn liquid hydrogen fuel cleanly. Liquefied hydrogen has only about one-quarter of the energy content of an equal volume of gasoline. But because hydrogen-fueled engines are more efficient, only about 9.5 liters (2.5 gallons) of hydrogen fuel would be needed to power a car the same distance as 3.8 liters (1 gallon) of gasoline. The prospect of clean, efficient vehicles has prompted carmakers around the world to manufacture prototype hydrogen-powered cars. The prospect of an unlimited source of energy in the future is prompting many to continue their work with hydrogen.

It should be pointed out, however, that hydrogen's use as a fuel or as a means of lifting balloons has already had negative effects on the human pop-

ulation, as well as on the environment. In 1937, the *Hindenburg*, a German dirigible that was filled with hydrogen, exploded over a crowd of onlookers at its mooring in Lakehurst, New Jersey, killing 35 of the 97 passengers aboard. In 1986, the U.S. space shuttle *Challenger* exploded 73 seconds after takeoff due to the mixing of leaking hydrogen and oxygen. While hydrogen does have excellent qualities as an alternative fuel, it is also a potentially dangerous substance, just as natural gas is, and must be contained and used in ways that will not bring harm to users and the environment.

TRASH-TO-ENERGY PROGRAMS

In spite of major efforts at recycling, particularly in developed countries, humans still generate billions of metric tons (billions of tons) of trash each year. Households, commercial and institutional facilities, and industry all contribute to this mountain of trash. Frequently called municipal solid waste, most of it is hauled off to landfills, where it decomposes over a period of many years. By using at least some of this trash to produce energy, communities could decrease their dependence on nonrenewable fossil fuels and at the same time lessen the amount of trash that has to enter landfills.

Unlike other forms of biomass, municipal solid waste must be collected and disposed of whether we use it for fuel or not. By building special "resource recovery" incinerators or gasification facilities, communities can use trash to produce energy. Some 200 communities in the United States have built resource recovery incinerators that burn trash to produce steam heat and/or electricity. A plant in Bridgeport, Connecticut, can burn more than 1,820 metric tons (2,000 tons) of trash per day. Steam produced by its boilers generates about 60 megawatts of electricity, enough to service about 60,000 homes.

Disadvantages and Environmental Impact. Burning solid wastes is not quite as easy as it sounds. Without costly separation, some of the material will not burn readily, sometimes simply because it is too wet. Valuable recyclable materials such as iron (Fe) or aluminum (Al) could end up in the waste, where

Trash–to–energy plants, like this one in Bermuda, burn solid waste while also generating steam or electricity. This procedure not only rids us of unrecycled waste but gives us usable energy.

they can be recovered, but with difficulty. In addition, combustion of solid wastes can produce air pollution and a significant amount of ash that must be safely disposed of. There is a possibility that toxic chemicals can be released into the air or end up in landfills with the ash. As with the combustion of fossil fuels, measures are being taken to reduce the risks associated with air pollutants and toxic wastes. But this method of producing energy is still considered more valuable as a means of trash disposal. Any useful energy generated is regarded as a plus.

Solid waste is also frequently disposed of in landfills, where the trash is spread out, compacted, and then covered with soil or sometimes with a concrete cap. After several years, the decomposition of the materials in a landfill provides another means of energy production. The decaying process produces methane gas. Methane, which is dangerous to breathe and can be explosive, may be tapped by drilling into the landfill. The methane can then be pumped out and piped to a generating plant where it can be used, like natural gas, to provide heat or produce electricity.

Energy production from trash is not particularly efficient. It takes large volumes of solid waste to produce a significant amount of energy. However, humans produce great quantities of trash every day.

FISSION AND FUSION

Fission. Nuclear power plants create a large amount of electricity from a small quantity of uranium (U) fuel, producing very few emissions in the process. These plants employ a process called nuclear fission. The nuclei of uranium atoms are split (fissioned), releasing energy and neutrons. The freed neutrons split other uranium atoms, creating a chain reaction that is capable of producing tremendous amounts of energy. Unfortunately, nuclear power plants have many inherent dangers, including the possibility of accidents that could release great amounts of radioactive material. And the problem of how to deal with the radioactive wastes from nuclear plants is yet to be solved. As a result, nuclear power plants face a great deal of public apprehension and opposition.

Fusion. In the meantime, scientists are working on another type of nuclear reaction—fusion. Instead of breaking large atoms into small atoms as fission does, fusion joins small atoms into larger ones. In fusion, the nuclei of two light atoms combine to form the nucleus of a heavier atom; in the process, there is a loss of mass and a release of tremendous energy. Fusion makes the Sun and stars burn and is the source of energy in hydrogen bombs. Fusion reactions can take place with deuterium, a naturally occurring isotope of hydrogen, one of the elements found in water. It has the potential for providing virtually unlimited energy. But fusion technology is extremely complex. To initiate fusion reactions, matter must be heated to millions of degrees Celsius (Fahrenheit). The high temperatures reduce the matter to an ionized gas called plasma. In the plasma, atomic particles acquire so much energy that they overcome their electrical repulsion and fuse. Once the energy is released, the process becomes self-sustaining and difficult to control. This is the challenge scientists face.

ENVIROBIT

By employing the process of fusion with two isotopes of hydrogen, deuterium and tritium, scientists estimate they could extract enough energy from the top 5 centimeters (2 inches) of water in Lake Erie to match the energy in all the world's oil reserves.

Numerous researchers have produced energy from fusion reactions. Scientists have been working for more than 20 years on a device called the Tokamak, which uses electromagnetic coils in the shape of a doughnut to create a magnetic field that squeezes and contains plasma. At the Princeton Plasma Physics Laboratory in New Jersey, a four-second experiment in 1993 produced more than 3 million watts of energy. Unfortunately, it consumed more than eight times that much energy to produce the high temperatures required for the reaction. Some scientists claim to have produced energy from what is being called cold fusion, a process that relies on electrochemical reactions at room temperatures. These efforts are still in the early stages and are being met with much skepticism. Nuclear fusion offers a great deal of potential—a virtually unlimited fuel supply. It remains to be seen whether the potential can be fulfilled.

COGENERATION

Cogeneration is a proven method of enhancing energy efficiency in industries as well as cities and towns. It is a process in which electricity is produced along with another form of usable energy, such as heat. Heat is trapped and used as an energy source to heat buildings or carry out more work, including the creation of even more electricity. Cogeneration is particularly useful for large buildings and energy-intensive industries. Most of these facilities require large amounts of electricity as well as energy for heating or cooling. Their electricity usually comes over transmission lines from a central power plant. There is a considerable amount of waste involved in this production and transmission of electricity. Meanwhile, the building itself contains a central furnace that burns more fuel to provide heating and cooling. Since the owners need the furnace anyway for heat, it could make sense for them to adapt it for creating electricity, too, as a low-cost "extra."

In a typical cogeneration facility, an electric generator is installed in the building. Fuel is burned in a boiler to produce steam that turns the generator. The waste heat from this combustion is used to heat the building or to drive air-conditioning units. Producing both heat and electricity from a single source saves from 10% to 30% of the fuel that would be required to produce them separately. The cost of electrical capacity from cogeneration systems is usually less than half the cost of a new coal- or nuclear-powered plant.

Cogeneration has been used to some extent since the late 1800s. In both Europe and the United States, many industrial sites once produced their own electricity. In 1900, more than half of the total American electrical-generating capacity was located at industrial sites. But as the demand for electricity grew and

reliable electric service was provided to more areas, on-site electric generation became less common.

In recent years, as the search has intensified for more efficient ways to use energy resources, there has been a renewed interest in cogeneration techniques. In 1978, a law was passed in the United States that requires electric utilities to purchase electricity produced by nonutility generators. This has encouraged some industries and even large apartment complexes to build cogeneration plants, selling any excess electricity they generate to the power companies. Not only do the plants provide independence from the prices charged by large electric utilities, they also free them from the possibility of power failures that sometimes strike centralized generating systems.

Cogeneration has the most potential in large industries such as chemical, pulp and paper, and food-processing plants as well as petroleum-refining and primary-metals industries. It can also be used successfully in hospitals, schools, office buildings, and apartment complexes. Less than 10% of electricity generated in the United States in 1990 was produced by cogeneration facilities. In some European countries, the percentage is much higher. In Denmark in 1991, for example, cogeneration accounted for more than 40% of the country's heating needs and more than 25% of its electricity.

GEOTHERMAL ENERGY

Geothermal energy is derived from heat stored within the Earth. It results from the radioactive decay of rocks, which raises Earth's temperature about 25°C (77°F) with each kilometer (0.62 mile) of depth. People have used heat from the Earth for thousands of years. In fact, the ancient Greeks, Romans and Japanese used hot springs for medicinal purposes and relaxation.

Since the early 1900s, geothermal energy has been used to heat buildings and provide warmth for all types of businesses from greenhouses to aquaculture. Geothermal heat is being used in places as diverse as Idaho, Italy, Japan, and Iceland. One limitation is that geothermal energy is available only at locations where heat from the Earth's interior is close enough to the surface to make its exploitation

The geysers and hot springs of places like Yellowstone National Park are one form of geothermal energy that occurs in nature. Here Old Faithful geyser in Yellowstone erupts on its regular schedule.

economically worthwhile. Where conditions are favorable, however, geothermal energy offers promise not only for economical space heating but also for the generation of electricity.

Tapping Geothermal Energy. Geothermal energy can be exploited in several ways. The most widely used method involves drilling down into hydrothermal reservoirs, underground pools where groundwater comes in contact with hot rock. If the temperature is high enough, the water may boil and turn into steam, which is used to power turbines that generate electricity. At the Geysers in California, located about 145 kilometers (90 miles) north of San Francisco, enough energy is produced to meet the needs of about 1.3 million people. In some cases, the temperature of the water underground is not hot enough to produce steam directly, but when the hot water is brought to the surface, some of it turns into steam because of the lower pressure at the surface. The steam may be used to generate electricity. Sometimes the heated water is used to boil other fluids with a boiling temperature lower than that of water. The steam produced in this way is then used to generate electricity.

ENVIROBIT

The Geysers geothermal plant in California generates about three-quarters of the total geothermal energy produced in the United States and provides about 7% of California's energy every year.

Most other methods of using geothermal energy are still in the experimental stage. One promising technique called hot dry rock (HDR) technology involves drilling wells into hot, dry rock and then pumping water down the well where it is heated and drawn out as steam to drive electric-generating turbines. This method could be widely used because it is not dependent on underground formations trapping and heating water. Many regions have hot, dry rock underground. If this form of

geothermal energy could be exploited, its energy-producing potential could be great.

Environmental Impact. Geothermal energy can cause pollution. One problem with geothermal energy is that the hot water contains corrosive salts. Also, if a large quantity of water is removed from beneath the ground and not replaced, the land could cave in. But as technology is developed to dig deep wells and to deal with the pollution problems, geothermal energy offers much promise for the future.

ETHANOL AND METHANOL

Ethanol and methanol are two types of alcohol that could be used as liquid fuels to help reduce the dependence on oil and damage to the environment. These fuels can either be substituted for, or added to, gasoline. When used in motor vehicles, these clean-burning fuels can substantially reduce pollution from their emissions. Both of these fuels can be produced from a variety of organic materials, including grains, sugar, and wood. Like other forms of biomass energy, ethanol and methanol are renewable resources.

Ethanol is a colorless, nearly odorless, flammable liquid produced by fermenting plant materials that are high in starches and sugars. Although most ethanol is made from corn, sorghum and sugarcane are also used and many other crops are being tested. Methanol can be produced from wood and other organic substances, including natural gas and coal. Converting these materials into usable fuels involves fermentation and distillation, processes similar to those used in producing alcoholic beverages. Yeasts are currently being used to aid fermentation, but research is under way to find other organisms, such as bacteria, that might accelerate the fermentation process. A great deal of energy is consumed and much waste produced in this process. Some of the waste, however, can be recycled and used as fertilizer. The production of ethanol and methanol is expensive. Without government tax incentives or subsidies, the cost of these fuels to consumers is currently too high.

The Clean Air Act amendments challenge power plants and other industries to produce cleaner emissions. This newer approach replaces the earlier attempt (shown here) to simply spread the pollution over a wider area by building tall smokestacks.

Brazil has led the way in the production of alcohol-based fuels. Spurred by the oil crisis of 1973, the country developed the world's largest ethanol-production effort. By 1985, nearly 4 million hectares (9.9 million acres) were devoted to sugarcane harvesting. By 1990, more than 11.4 billion liters (3 billion gallons) of ethanol were being produced. Eight million cars run on a blend of gasoline and ethanol, and Brazil's automobile industry now manufactures cars with engines that can run on pure ethanol. While Brazil's investment in the ethanol industry has been substantial—more than $5 billion—the country has saved more than that by not having to purchase foreign oil.

ENVIROBIT

Alcohol fuels from sugarcane provide about one-half of Brazil's automotive fuel.

The 1970s oil crisis also prompted the United States to establish an alcohol-based fuel program. Encouraged by tax breaks and other government subsidies, farmers in many states began to grow huge crops of corn, sugarcane, and sorghum. Production of ethanol increased from around 757 million liters (200 million gallons) in 1981 to nearly 3.4 billion liters (900 million gallons) by 1990. States with pollution problems have begun looking to ethanol and methanol as alternative sources of fuel. The use of an alcohol mix in fuels is required in the Denver area, for example, to help cut down on carbon monoxide emissions in the winter. Gasohol, a blend of 90% gasoline and 10% ethanol, is being sold in an increasing number of states.

Disadvantages and Environmental Impact. There are disadvantages associated with these fuels. Ethanol and methanol can be somewhat corrosive and are easily contaminated by water. They are more costly than gasoline. Cars running on these fuels or on gasoline-alcohol mixtures get fewer kilometers (miles) per gallon than cars running on 100% gasoline. In some countries, it is feared that production of fuel crops could someday compete with the production of food. Recent concerns have also been raised about preserving the biodiversity of Earth. Huge plantations devoted to fuel-producing crops could threaten the existence of many other species. Proponents of alcohol-based fuels say conflicts like these could be avoided by relying more on wood and agricultural wastes, such as corncobs and rice hulls. This tactic would also reduce the cost of producing these potentially valuable fuels.

CLEANING THE AIR

The energy crisis of the 1970s and early 1980s has not gone away, but it has been overshadowed in many respects by a growing concern about the environmental effects of human energy use. Environmental pollution affects not only individual nations but the entire world. The use of fossil fuels has contributed greatly to air pollution in particular. By turning away from fossil fuels and toward renewable resources, humans can work to solve both energy problems and environmental crises.

Full-Cost Pricing. One innovative proposal to deal with air pollution and energy problems involves what is called full-cost pricing. Currently, most renewable resources, in the early stages of technology development, are simply too expensive to be pursued on a broad scale. Fossil fuels, with their ready availability and low prices, are easy to choose. However, if the cost of treating the air-pollution problems that fossil fuels cause were added to their market price, many alternative fuels would become much more cost-competitive. Fossil fuels and renewable energy resources have not been competing on the same level in the marketplace. Once installed, renewable energy systems require no costly fuel and produce very little pollution. If these factors were considered, renewable resources would be comparable in cost to fossil fuels.

Clean Air Act. In 1970, the United States passed the Clean Air Act in an effort to control air pollution. The act, along with its subsequent amendments, classified the most widespread and dangerous pollutants and established strict standards as to how much of each may be present in the air. The act focused both on limiting emissions from power plants and other industries, and on forcing automobile manufacturers to produce cleaner, more fuel-efficient cars. As a result, levels of the Environmental Protection Agency's six key health-related air pollutants have been reduced—lead (Pb), carbon monoxide (CO), sulfur dioxide (SO_2), particulate matter, nitrogen oxide (NO), and ozone (O_3). Although air quality improved dramatically in the decades following the passage of the Clean Air Act, it was estimated in 1990 that 90 million people in the United States still lived in areas that failed to meet federal standards.

Sweeping amendments to the original Clean Air Act were passed in 1990. A portion of these amendments focuses on those areas that have not yet met air-quality standards and on developing plans for individual states to bring these locales into compliance. A major focus of the amendments is on automobile emissions. Even though each of today's cars individually produces significantly less pollution than cars of the 1960s, overall pollution from vehicle emissions has not much improved. This can be attributed primarily to the fact that there are more cars on the road today. The 1990 amendments require cleaner fuels and cleaner-burning cars as well as fewer particulate emissions from diesel-fueled trucks and buses. They include specific requirements for emission inspection and maintenance programs in many metropolitan areas. The smoggiest metropolitan areas will have to institute policies that discourage unnecessary automobile use and encourage efficient commuting, such as van pools and high-occupancy vehicle (HOV) lanes. Surcharges may even be added to parking fees.

Acid-rain-forming pollutants from power plants also received major scrutiny in the Clean Air Act amendments of 1990. Sulfur dioxide emissions from these plants are to be reduced to mandated levels by the year 2000. The Environmental Protection Agency (EPA) is now issuing one permit per 0.91 metric ton (1 ton) of sulfur dioxide released from a smokestack. If a plant expects to release more sulfur dioxide than the amount of permits the EPA will allow them, the company will have to purchase additional allowances from another, cleaner plant that will not emit its entire allotment. This system is called emissions credit trading. The permits are called tradable permits, marketable permits, or sometimes emissions permits. Plants will also have to install continuous emission monitoring systems, which keep track of how much sulfur dioxide and nitrogen oxides are released.

The standards established in the United States by the Clean Air Act and its amendments are some of the toughest in the world. Standards set in more-developed countries may be of little immediate interest to lesser-developed nations that are still dealing with basic sanitation problems such as contaminated water due to lack of sewage treatment. Even in more-developed areas, the cost of meeting pollution standards can be overwhelming to fragile economies. Poland, for example, is anxious to join the European Community (EC), a government composed of representatives from many European Nations. In order to meet the environmental standards set by the EC, the Polish government estimates it will have to spend more than $250 billion.

International Attention. There have been numerous international conferences on the environment whose programs have focused on measures to improve air quality. The 1987 Montreal Protocol and ensuing 1990 London Amendments are landmark agreements that aim to phase out the use of ozone-depleting substances. However, only a limited number of nations ratified the agreements. In May 1992, the United Nations Framework Convention on Climate Change was adopted and signed initially by more than 150 countries. It calls for stabilization of greenhouse gas concentrations at levels that will prevent interference with the climate. The effort requires that countries make plans to deal with carbon dioxide emissions but recognizes that developing countries, in particular, may have other, predominant priorities, such as the eradication of poverty. To achieve clean air for the entire planet requires a global commitment, but local actions must be undertaken to see this commitment through.

ENERGY EFFICIENCY

Improving energy efficiency is a grave environmental issue. It can result in immediate savings of money and resources. Every barrel of oil not used today is saved for tomorrow. After the oil crisis of 1973, many industrialized nations pursued strategies of conservation and energy efficiency. The savings amounted to billions of barrels of oil. The technology to improve efficiency can take the form of compact fluorescent light bulbs or industrial motors with adjustable-speed drives. Energy efficiency can be achieved by homeowners, industries, utilities, and governments.

In 1983, the United States consumed less energy than it did in 1973. This occurred despite the fact that the economy and the population grew and the U.S. produced more goods and services in 1983 than a decade earlier. Similar progress was made in many industrialized nations. For the first time in history, the economy was able to expand without a corresponding increase in the amount of energy consumed. Many large companies now have energy managers whose role is to find ways to produce more of a product with less energy and materials. More attention to efficient methods, use of state-of-the-art motors, and improved sensors and instrumentation as well as better management of waste heat can result in better maintenance procedures. Recycling materials can save vast amounts of energy as well. In the United States, the EPA's "Green Lights Program" encourages widespread use of energy-efficient lighting in businesses and public institutions. If fully implemented, the EPA envisions a potential savings of $16 billion in electricity costs.

Public utilities already offer incentives for those taking part in such energy-conservation programs. They could further improve energy efficiency by setting rate structures that encourage customers to save electricity rather than use more. Some utilities offer incentives to customers who voluntarily agree to have their air conditioners shut off for short periods during the hottest weather. Through programs like this, utilities can avoid building new power plants just to meet peak demands. Governments, too, can offer incentives for more efficient use of energy. Higher gasoline taxes, while extremely controversial, may reduce pollution and oil dependency.

It would be beneficial for industrialized nations to share their experience with lesser-developed countries. Historically, early stages of development involve the most wasteful consumption of energy. By allowing developing countries to make use of energy-efficient technologies as they expand their economies, less fuel may be wasted and fewer pollutants will be added to the environment.

THE IMPORTANCE OF CONSERVATION

There is more technology enabling us to use energy more efficiently than ever before. If the technology is not used, however, and if individuals don't develop a conservation mentality, energy will continue to be wasted.

There are many opportunities to save energy in the day-to-day operation of a household. Investment in weather-stripping, insulation, automatic thermostats, and energy-efficient light bulbs means less consumption of fossils fuels and fewer dollars spent in the long run. Energy-efficiency ratings on major appliances convey important information. Making a choice based on energy efficiency can result in substantial energy savings.

ENVIROBIT

To heat rooms to a temperature of 20°C (68°F) and water to a temperature of 60°C (140°F), a high-energy flame with a temperature of more than 1,000°C (1,832°F) is usually used.

In the same way, buying a fuel-efficient car can save thousands of liters of gasoline over a relatively short time. Car owners might also try to develop new attitudes toward using their automobiles. Few can give them up altogether, but by commuting by van pool or public transportation, fossil fuels could be conserved and emissions reduced. Telecommuting from home, or commuting to work electronically, would save on-the-road commuting time and fuel. It would also reduce the congestion on overcrowded highways.

ENVIROBIT

According to the U.S. Environmental Protection Agency, increasing mass transit ridership by 10% in the five largest metropolitan areas would save 511 million liters (135 million gallons) of gasoline a year.

Recycling is another way individuals can help conserve energy and save resources. Manufacturing products from new materials can require substantially more energy than producing them from recycled materials. Recycling household materials may not provide an immediate financial reward reflected in a utility bill or a monthly budget. As with most conservation techniques, the benefits will be seen in the long term and will eventually touch industries, nations, and the world.

Energy conservation requires a personal commitment. It frequently involves small steps that an individual takes to save energy at home, at work, and on the road. Many of these steps seem trivial, but if enough individuals walk in the same direction, conservation can make a difference for the future of humankind and the planet Earth.

Sources

Corson, Walter, ed. *The Global Ecology Handbook*. Boston: Beacon Press, 1990.

Golob, Richard, and Eric Brus. *The Almanac of Renewable Energy*. New York: Henry Holt, World Information Systems, 1993.

Nebel, Bernard J. *Environmental Science: The Way the World Works*. 2nd ed. Englewood Cliffs, NJ: Prentice-Hall, 1987.

Schwartz, A. Truman, et al. *Chemistry in Context*. Dubuque, I.A.: Wm. C. Brown Publishers, 1994. ©American Chemical Society.

World Energy Council. *Energy for Tomorrow's World*. New York: St. Martin's Press, 1993.

World Resources Institute. *The 1994 Information Please Environmental Almanac*. Boston: Houghton Mifflin Co., 1994.

Index